Contents

OXFORD STUDENT TEXTS

Series Editor: Victor Lee

Geoffrey Chaucer

General Prologue to The Canterbury Tales

Edited by Peter Mack and Chris Walton

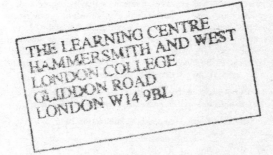

Oxford University Press

OXFORD
UNIVERSITY PRESS

Great Clarendon Street, Oxford OX2 6DP

Oxford University Press is a department of the University of Oxford.
It furthers the University's objective of excellence in research, scholarship,
and education by publishing worldwide in

Oxford   New York

Auckland   Cape Town   Dar es Salaam   Hong Kong   Karachi
Kuala Lumpur   Madrid   Melbourne   Mexico City   Nairobi
New Delhi   Shanghai   Taipei   Toronto

With offices in

Argentina   Austria   Brazil   Chile   Czech Republic   France   Greece
Guatemala   Hungary   Italy   Japan   South Korea   Poland   Portugal
Singapore   Switzerland   Thailand   Turkey   Ukraine   Vietnam

Oxford is a registered trade mark of Oxford University Press
in the UK and in certain other countries

British Library Cataloguing in Publication Data

Data available

ISBN: 978-0-19-832876-6

1 3 5 7 9 10 8 6 4 2

Typeset in Goudy Old Style MT by
Palimpsest Book Production Limited, Grangemouth, Stirlingshire

Printed in Great Britain by CPI Cox & Wyman, Reading, RG1 8EX

Paper used in the production of this book is a natural, recyclable product made from wood
grown in sustainable forests. The manufacturing process conforms to the environmental
regulations of the country of origin

The publishers would like to thank the following for permission to reproduce
photographs: Mary Evans Picture Library and Oxford University Press

Acknowledgements

Peter Mack would like to acknowledge the help he received in compiling the notes from the critical works and editions listed in Further Reading, and from his colleagues, Gloria Cigman and Bill Whitehead. He is grateful to Robert Burchfield for his comments on the Note on Chaucer's English. Chris Walton would like to thank Claire Fidler and his A level students for their comments on the Interpretations, Erica Holley for valuable historical resources, and Barbara Mitchell for providing critical material. Both editors would like to thank Victor Lee, Lucy Hooper and Jan Doorly for their constructive criticism and advice.

The text is taken from *The Riverside Chaucer*, Third Edition, edited by Larry D. Benson, copyright © 1987 by Houghton Mifflin Company.

Editors

Dr Victor Lee, the series editor, read English at University College, Cardiff. He was later awarded his doctorate at the University of Oxford. He has taught at secondary and tertiary level, working at the Open University for 27 years. Victor Lee's experience as an examiner is very wide. He has been, for example, a Chief Examiner in English A level for three different boards, stretching over a period of more than 30 years.

Professor Peter Mack read English at St Peter's College, Oxford, and went on to gain an MPhil and PhD in Renaissance Studies from the Warburg Institute, University of London. He has examined English at GCSE and A level as well as for the International Baccalaureate. He has been editor of the journal *Rhetorica* and head of the English Department at the University of Warwick, where he has taught Medieval English Studies since 1979. His books include *Renaissance Argument* (1993), *Renaissance Rhetoric* (1994) and *Elizabethan Rhetoric* (2002).

Chris Walton read English Literature and Philosophy at Leeds University and gained an MPhil in classroom research from Bath University. He has taught A level English and English Literature for over 30 years and has written modular specifications in the subjects. He has published revision and study guides for GCSE and A level. After working as a headteacher, he is currently developing reforms in the 14–19 curriculum for Swindon and he is also a registered School Improvement Partner in the secondary sector.

Foreword

Oxford Student Texts are specifically aimed at presenting poetry and drama to an audience studying English literature at an advanced level. Each text is designed as an integrated whole consisting of four main parts. The first part sets the scene by discussing the context in which the work was written. The most important part of the book is the poetry or play itself, and it is suggested that the student read this first without consulting the Notes or other secondary sources. To encourage students to follow this advice, the Notes are placed together after the text, not alongside it. Where help is needed, the Notes and Interpretations sections provide it.

The Notes perform two functions. First, they provide information and explain allusions. Second (this is where they differ from most texts at this level), they often raise questions of central concern to the interpretation of the poetry or play being dealt with, particularly in the general note placed at the beginning of each set of notes.

The fourth part, the Interpretations section, deals with major issues of response to the particular selection of poetry or drama. One of the major aims of this part of the text is to emphasize that there is no one right answer to interpretation, but a series of approaches. Readers are given guidance as to what counts as evidence, but in the end left to make up their own minds as to which are the most suitable interpretations, or to add their own.

In these revised editions, the Interpretations section now addresses a wider range of issues. There is a more detailed treatment of context and critical history, for example. The section contains a number of activity-discussion sequences, although it must be stressed that these are optional. Significant issues about the poetry or play are raised, and readers are invited to tackle activities before proceeding to the discussion section, where possible responses to the questions raised are considered. Their main function is to engage readers actively in the ideas of the text.

At the end of each text there is also a list of Essay Questions. Whereas the activity-discussion sequences are aimed at increasing understanding of the literary work itself, these tasks are intended to help explore ideas about the poetry or play after the student has completed the reading of the work and the studying of the Notes and Interpretations. These tasks are particularly helpful for coursework projects or in preparing for an examination.

Victor Lee *Series Editor*

Chaucer's *General Prologue* in Context

Conditions of writing

During Chaucer's lifetime (c. 1343–1400) and for two centuries afterwards, it was impossible to make a living by writing. In order to support themselves writers needed other jobs (Chaucer worked as a diplomat and a civil servant; some other writers worked as priests) and patronage, which usually took the form of gifts of money in return for the dedication of a poem or book, or the gift of a manuscript copy. The only people with the financial resources to provide writers with patronage were the king, the great barons of the realm and, increasingly in the fourteenth and fifteenth centuries, wealthy London merchants.

Chaucer was the son of a London wine merchant, in whose house he would have learned to read and write English and French. He may also have learned Italian from his father's business associates. At school he learned Latin, which was the language of learning and of much international communication, and rhetoric (the art of speaking and writing effectively). He would also have read widely in Latin poetry. In 1357, at the age of about 14, Chaucer became a page in the household of Elizabeth, Countess of Ulster, and Prince Lionel, King Edward III's second son, and in 1359 he was sent to France as a squire in the English army. So Chaucer combined a London mercantile origin and basic education with the training and early manhood experiences of a courtier.

In the fourteenth century it was relatively expensive to obtain a manuscript (and of course manuscripts were the only kind of books before the invention of printing around 1465). Usually you had to borrow a copy of the work you wanted, buy parchment and ink, and hire a scribe to copy it out for you. Some booksellers hired scribes to make ready-to-buy copies of books they thought would sell, but the cost of this service was higher.

Few people knew how to read or had the leisure to do so. In great courts a poet might read from his book to the nobles, their feudal supporters and their servants. The feudal system of land tenure meant that great lords held their lands in return for military service to and attendance on the king. In the same way, lesser feudal lords would owe service to their superiors and expect service and attendance from the knights and squires dependent on them.

Some merchant families would have owned books only for business, for example law books or books connected with a trade, or religious books, for the important purpose of saving their souls. Those who were sufficiently wealthy to afford books for leisure may have imitated courtly practice with after-meal readings of poetry to the whole family, or family members may have read to themselves.

Because the main sources of patronage were aristocratic, non-religious literature tends to employ aristocratic forms, like the romance, and to uphold aristocratic values. Since the great merchants aspired to (and sometimes did) join the aristocracy, they would have followed aristocratic tastes, but they (and especially lesser merchants) may have been more willing to entertain mockery or criticism of, for example, aristocratic complacency and idleness. Although merchants, like Chaucer's father, made much of their money from paid service to the king and nobles, their position was ultimately reliant on the financial profits they could make. They were both partly independent of the state and more reliant than aristocrats on their own ability to respond quickly to the challenges and opportunities of the international market.

There is some manuscript and historical evidence that whereas Chaucer's earlier poems, such as *The Book of the Duchess* and *Troilus and Criseyde*, were directed to royal or aristocratic patrons, *The Canterbury Tales*, which he wrote towards the end of his career and left incomplete at his death, was intended for a London business audience. This would have been a good reason

A woodcut based on a portrait miniature of Chaucer from the
Ellesmere manuscript of *The Canterbury Tales*

for adding representatives of various trades to the pilgrims, as he
does in the *General Prologue*. For a courtly audience it would have
seemed strange to write about a large group of people which
included only one knight and his squire.

Holiday

The pilgrimage to Canterbury is presented as an escape from the
world of work and duty. Some are making the journey for the
sake of amusement, some for the health of their souls; most,
probably, are motivated by a combination of the two. Usually,
lower-class medieval people were only given time off work for
religious feast days. They needed to make the best of these
holidays for amusement as well as in order to save their souls.
Provided that proper respect was paid to religious observance,
the Church and civic authorities recognized that holy days also
gave opportunities for the satisfaction of human needs for
relaxation, companionship and enjoyment.

The long holiday of the pilgrimage was unavailable to serfs, the rural poor and waged craftsmen, who made up the majority of the population but remained largely invisible to literature. Chaucer's pilgrimage is firmly located in the spring, a season of relief and reawakening after the long winter, and the more independent middle layer of society form the majority of the pilgrims.

The journey is unlike normal fourteenth-century social situations because of the range of social classes who have joined together in a state of near equality (under the direction of the Host) for mutual protection on the road and to enjoy the stories which different pilgrims will tell. They will compete against each other to win the prize for the best tale (a free supper offered by the Host), but they collaborate to promote safety and pleasure. For the duration of the pilgrimage the lowest ranking pilgrims, such as the Miller and the Shipman, will have as much right to be heard and as much scope for cajoling or persuading others to defer to their wishes as the Knight and the Squire.

The *General Prologue* celebrates the material and cultural richness of late fourteenth-century life: the pilgrims' clothes and possessions, the food they eat, the books they have read, the names of the places across Europe and the Middle East where they have prayed or traded or fought. Chaucer shows eminent respect for religion in his portrayal of the Parson as an ideally caring shepherd of his flock, and his brother the Ploughman is a model of hard-working lay piety, but several of the strongest portraits focus on the problems of reconciling religious profession with the demands and temptations of life in the material world. The Monk loves hunting and eating so much that he barely has time for saying his services and his prayers; the supposedly celibate Friar pays off his mistresses with the donations he receives from satisfied penitents; the Pardoner grossly deceives the audiences of his sermons in order to make a profit on his license to preach and to sell indulgences. The *General Prologue* explores the social and personal consequences of the difficulty of reconciling religion, money and pleasure.

Canterbury pilgrims on the road, from an image first published in 1387

Satire and judgement

From the literary point of view, Chaucer's decision to begin *The Canterbury Tales* with descriptions of the 30 travellers who formed the company seems bold to the point of recklessness. How could the original listeners or later readers be expected to take an interest in and remember so many people? In fact, Chaucer sustains our interest by the variety of the portraits and the surprises that each of them contains. What might have been expected to be problematic in fact became one of his greatest and most original successes.

Jill Mann (see Further Reading, page 166) showed that Chaucer's bold move involved using a particular medieval genre called 'estates satire' as the introduction to his collection of narratives (another well-established kind of book). Medieval society was divided into three 'estates': nobles, religious and

5

commons. Estates satire was typically hierarchical, conservative and judgemental, confronting occupation groups representing each of the three estates with the gap between the high ideals applying to their profession and its present corruption. It tended to call for a return to proper observance of religious and secular rules.

Chaucer's *General Prologue* retains the naming of occupation groups (and consequently the severe under-representation of women) and even some of the specific criticisms, but the rules for the representatives of particular groups are generally implied rather than stated, and the tone is much less condemnatory. So, for instance, we can deduce from Chaucer's descriptions of their interests that the Monk and the Prioress are not really following the rules applying to their status, but Chaucer's comments tend to be approving of their actions and sometimes apparently even questioning of the rules. Where other medieval writers would be angry at the hypocrisy of the people being described, Chaucer appears to be amused by human folly and forgiving of understandable human weakness, even in the case of downright rogues. Derek Pearsall (see Further Reading, page 166) has suggested that readers are put in the position of being invited to use their knowledge of how people ought to behave to make judgements against the pilgrims, but at the same time being made to feel that 'the urge to disapprove is unduly harsh' (*The Canterbury Tales*, page 68).

The subject of the *General Prologue*, with its portraits of the activities, interests and foibles of so many different professions, is medieval society, but social-group criticism is balanced by the flashes of individuality which Chaucer approvingly records: the jingling bells on the Monk's bridle, the Wife of Bath's self-sufficiency and openness to experience, the Friar's twinkling eyes, the uneducated Manciple's practical intelligence, and the Pardoner's singing, for example. Chaucer's descriptions take delight in the pleasures open equally to all his middle-ranking pilgrims: music, food, clothes and company.

General Prologue to The Canterbury Tales

Here bygynneth the Book of the Tales of Caunterbury.

Whan that Aprill with his shoures soote
The droghte of March hath perced to the roote,
And bathed every veyne in swich licour
Of which vertu engendred is the flour;
5   Whan Zephirus eek with his sweete breeth
Inspired hath in every holt and heeth
The tendre croppes, and the yonge sonne
Hath in the Ram his half cours yronne,
And smale foweles maken melodye,
10   That slepen al the nyght with open ye
(So priketh hem nature in hir corages),
Thanne longen folk to goon on pilgrimages,
And palmeres for to seken straunge strondes,
To ferne halwes, kowthe in sondry londes;
15   And specially from every shires ende
Of Engelond to Caunterbury they wende,
The hooly blisful martir for to seke,
That hem hath holpen whan that they were seeke.
Bifil that in that seson on a day,
20   In Southwerk at the Tabard as I lay
Redy to wenden on my pilgrymage
To Caunterbury with ful devout corage,
At nyght was come into that hostelrye
Wel nyne and twenty in a compaignye
25   Of sondry folk, by aventure yfalle
In felaweshipe, and pilgrimes were they alle,
That toward Caunterbury wolden ryde.
The chambres and the stables weren wyde,

And wel we weren esed atte beste.
30   And shortly, whan the sonne was to reste,
So hadde I spoken with hem everichon
That I was of hir felaweshipe anon,
And made forward erly for to ryse,
To take oure wey ther as I yow devyse.
35   But nathelees, whil I have tyme and space,
Er that I ferther in this tale pace,
Me thynketh it acordaunt to resoun
To telle yow al the condicioun
Of ech of hem, so as it semed me,
40   And whiche they weren, and of what degree,
And eek in what array that they were inne;
And at a knyght than wol I first bigynne.
       A KNYGHT ther was, and that a worthy man,
That fro the tyme that he first bigan
45   To riden out, he loved chivalrie,
Trouthe and honour, fredom and curteisie.
Ful worthy was he in his lordes werre,
And therto hadde he riden, no man ferre,
As wel in cristendom as in hethenesse,
50   And evere honoured for his worthynesse;
At Alisaundre he was whan it was wonne.
Ful ofte tyme he hadde the bord bigonne
Aboven alle nacions in Pruce;
In Lettow hadde he reysed and in Ruce,
55   No Cristen man so ofte of his degree.
In Gernade at the seege eek hadde he be
Of Algezir, and riden in Belmarye.
At Lyeys was he and at Satalye,
Whan they were wonne, and in the Grete See
60   At many a noble armee hadde he be.
At mortal batailles hadde he been fiftene,
And foughten for oure feith at Tramyssene

In lystes thries, and ay slayn his foo.
This ilke worthy knyght hadde been also
65 Somtyme with the lord of Palatye
Agayn another hethen in Turkye;
And everemoore he hadde a sovereyn prys.
And though that he were worthy, he was wys,
And of his port as meeke as is a mayde.
70 He nevere yet no vileynye ne sayde
In al his lyf unto no maner wight.
He was a verray, parfit gentil knyght.
But for to tellen yow of his array,
His hors were goode, but he was nat gay.
75 Of fustian he wered a gypon
Al bismotered with his habergeon,
For he was late ycome from his viage,
And wente for to doon his pilgrymage.
     With hym ther was his sone, a yong SQUIER,
80 A lovyere and a lusty bacheler,
With lokkes crulle as they were leyd in presse.
Of twenty yeer of age he was, I gesse.
Of his stature he was of evene lengthe,
And wonderly delyvere, and of greet strengthe.
85 And he hadde been somtyme in chyvachie
In Flaundres, in Artoys, and Pycardie,
And born hym weel, as of so litel space,
In hope to stonden in his lady grace.
Embrouded was he, as it were a meede
90 Al ful of fresshe floures, whyte and reede.
Syngynge he was, or floytynge, al the day;
He was as fressh as is the month of May.
Short was his gowne, with sleves longe and wyde.
Wel koude he sitte on hors and faire ryde.
95 He koude songes make and wel endite,
Juste and eek daunce, and weel purtreye and write.

So hoote he lovede that by nyghtertale
He sleep namoore than dooth a nyghtyngale.
Curteis he was, lowely, and servysable,
100 And carf biforn his fader at the table.
    A YEMAN hadde he and servantz namo
At that tyme, for hym liste ride so,
And he was clad in cote and hood of grene.
A sheef of pecok arwes, bright and kene,
105 Under his belt he bar ful thriftily
(Wel koude he dresse his takel yemanly;
His arwes drouped noght with fetheres lowe),
And in his hand he baar a myghty bowe.
A not heed hadde he, with a broun visage.
110 Of wodecraft wel koude he al the usage.
Upon his arm he baar a gay bracer,
And by his syde a swerd and a bokeler,
And on that oother syde a gay daggere
Harneised wel and sharp as point of spere;
115 A Cristopher on his brest of silver sheene.
An horn he bar, the bawdryk was of grene;
A forster was he, soothly, as I gesse.
    Ther was also a Nonne, a PRIORESSE,
That of hir smylyng was ful symple and coy;
120 Hire gretteste ooth was but by Seinte Loy;
And she was cleped madame Eglentyne.
Ful weel she soong the service dyvyne,
Entuned in hir nose ful semely;
And Frenssh she spak ful faire and fetisly,
125 After the scole of Stratford atte Bowe,
For Frenssh of Parys was to hire unknowe.
At mete wel ytaught was she with alle;
She leet no morsel from hir lippes falle,
Ne wette hir fyngres in hir sauce depe;
130 Wel koude she carie a morsel and wel kepe

That no drope ne fille upon hire brest.
In curteisie was set ful muchel hir lest.
Hir over-lippe wyped she so clene
That in hir coppe ther was no ferthyng sene
135 Of grece, whan she dronken hadde hir draughte.
Ful semely after hir mete she raughte.
And sikerly she was of greet desport,
And ful plesaunt, and amyable of port,
And peyned hire to countrefete cheere
140 Of court, and to been estatlich of manere,
And to ben holden digne of reverence.
But for to speken of hire conscience,
She was so charitable and so pitous
She wolde wepe, if that she saugh a mous
145 Kaught in a trappe, if it were deed or bledde.
Of smale houndes hadde she that she fedde
With rosted flessh, or milk and wastel-breed.
But soore wepte she if oon of hem were deed,
Or if men smoot it with a yerde smerte;
150 And al was conscience and tendre herte.
Ful semyly hir wympul pynched was,
Hir nose tretys, hir eyen greye as glas,
Hir mouth ful smal, and therto softe and reed.
But sikerly she hadde a fair forheed;
155 It was almoost a spanne brood, I trowe;
For, hardily, she was nat undergrowe.
Ful fetys was hir cloke, as I was war.
Of smal coral aboute hire arm she bar
A peire of bedes, gauded al with grene,
160 And theron heng a brooch of gold ful sheene,
On which ther was first write a crowned A,
And after *Amor vincit omnia.*
      Another NONNE with hire hadde she,
That was hir chapeleyne, and preestes thre.

165 A MONK ther was, a fair for the maistrie,
  An outridere, that lovede venerie,
  A manly man, to been an abbot able.
  Ful many a deyntee hors hadde he in stable,
  And whan he rood, men myghte his brydel heere
170 Gynglen in a whistlynge wynd als cleere
  And eek as loude as dooth the chapel belle
  Ther as this lord was kepere of the celle.
  The reule of Seint Maure or of Seint Beneit –
  By cause that it was old and somdel streit
175 This ilke Monk leet olde thynges pace,
  And heeld after the newe world the space.
  He yaf nat of that text a pulled hen,
  That seith that hunters ben nat hooly men,
  Ne that a monk, whan he is recchelees,
180 Is likned til a fissh that is waterlees –
  This is to seyn, a monk out of his cloystre.
  But thilke text heeld he nat worth an oystre;
  And I seyde his opinion was good.
  What sholde he studie and make hymselven wood,
185 Upon a book in cloystre alwey to poure,
  Or swynken with his handes, and laboure,
  As Austyn bit? How shal the world be served?
  Lat Austyn have his swynk to hym reserved!
  Therfore he was a prikasour aright:
190 Grehoundes he hadde as swift as fowel in flight;
  Of prikyng and of huntyng for the hare
  Was al his lust, for no cost wolde he spare.
  I seigh his sleves purfiled at the hond
  With grys, and that the fyneste of a lond;
195 And for to festne his hood under his chyn,
  He hadde of gold ywroght a ful curious pyn;
  A love-knotte in the gretter ende ther was.
  His heed was balled, that shoon as any glas,

And eek his face, as he hadde been enoynt.
200 He was a lord ful fat and in good poynt;
His eyen stepe, and rollynge in his heed,
That stemed as a forneys of a leed;
His bootes souple, his hors in greet estaat.
Now certeinly he was a fair prelaat;
205 He was nat pale as a forpyned goost.
A fat swan loved he best of any roost.
His palfrey was as broun as is a berye.
    A FRERE ther was, a wantowne and a merye,
A lymytour, a ful solempne man.
210 In alle the ordres foure is noon that kan
So muchel of daliaunce and fair langage.
He hadde maad ful many a mariage
Of yonge wommen at his owene cost.
Unto his ordre he was a noble post.
215 Ful wel biloved and famulier was he
With frankeleyns over al in his contree,
And eek with worthy wommen of the toun;
For he hadde power of confessioun,
As seyde hymself, moore than a curat,
220 For of his ordre he was licenciat.
Ful swetely herde he confessioun,
And plesaunt was his absolucioun:
He was an esy man to yeve penaunce,
Ther as he wiste to have a good pitaunce.
225 For unto a povre ordre for to yive
Is signe that a man is wel yshryve;
For if he yaf, he dorste make avaunt,
He wiste that a man was repentaunt;
For many a man so hard is of his herte,
230 He may nat wepe, althogh hym soore smerte.
Therfore in stede of wepynge and preyeres
Men moote yeve silver to the povre freres.

His typet was ay farsed ful of knyves
And pynnes, for to yeven faire wyves.
235 And certeinly he hadde a murye note:
Wel koude he synge and pleyen on a rote;
Of yeddynges he baar outrely the pris.
His nekke whit was as the flour-de-lys;
Therto he strong was as a champioun.
240 He knew the tavernes wel in every toun
And everich hostiler and tappestere
Bet than a lazar or a beggestere,
For unto swich a worthy man as he
Acorded nat, as by his facultee,
245 To have with sike lazars aqueyntaunce.
It is nat honest; it may nat avaunce,
For to deelen with no swich poraille,
But al with riche and selleres of vitaille.
And over al, ther as profit sholde arise,
250 Curteis he was and lowely of servyse;
Ther nas no man nowher so vertuous.
He was the beste beggere in his hous;
252ᵃ [And yaf a certeyn ferme for the graunt;
252ᵇ Noon of his bretheren cam ther in his haunt;]
For thogh a wydwe hadde noght a sho,
So plesaunt was his 'In principio',
255 Yet wolde he have a ferthyng, er he wente.
His purchas was wel bettre than his rente.
And rage he koude, as it were right a whelp.
In love-dayes ther koude he muchel help,
For ther he was nat lyk a cloysterer
260 With a thredbare cope, as is a povre scoler,
But he was lyk a maister or a pope.
Of double worstede was his semycope,
That rounded as a belle out of the presse.
Somwhat he lipsed, for his wantownesse,

265 To make his Englissh sweete upon his tonge;
And in his harpyng, whan that he hadde songe,
His eyen twynkled in his heed aryght
As doon the sterres in the frosty nyght.
This worthy lymytour was cleped Huberd.

270   A MARCHANT was ther with a forked berd,
In mottelee, and hye on horse he sat;
Upon his heed a Flaundryssh bever hat,
His bootes clasped faire and fetisly.
His resons he spak ful solempnely,

275 Sownynge alwey th'encrees of his wynnyng.
He wolde the see were kept for any thyng
Bitwixe Middelburgh and Orewelle.
Wel koude he in eschaunge sheeldes selle.
This worthy man ful wel his wit bisette:

280 Ther wiste no wight that he was in dette,
So estatly was he of his governaunce
With his bargaynes and with his chevyssaunce.
For sothe he was a worthy man with alle,
But, sooth to seyn, I noot how men hym calle.

285   A CLERK ther was of Oxenford also,
That unto logyk hadde longe ygo.
As leene was his hors as is a rake,
And he nas nat right fat, I undertake,
But looked holwe, and therto sobrely.

290 Ful thredbare was his overeste courtepy,
For he hadde geten hym yet no benefice,
Ne was so worldly for to have office.
For hym was levere have at his beddes heed
Twenty bookes, clad in blak or reed,

295 Of Aristotle and his philosophie
Than robes riche, or fithele, or gay sautrie.
But al be that he was a philosophre,
Yet hadde he but litel gold in cofre;

But al that he myghte of his freendes hente,
300 On bookes and on lernynge he it spente,
And bisily gan for the soules preye
Of hem that yaf hym wherwith to scoleye.
Of studie took he moost cure and moost heede.
Noght o word spak he moore than was neede,
305 And that was seyd in forme and reverence,
And short and quyk and ful of hy sentence;
Sownynge in moral vertu was his speche,
And gladly wolde he lerne and gladly teche.
    A SERGEANT OF THE LAWE, war and wys,
310 That often hadde been at the Parvys,
Ther was also, ful riche of excellence.
Discreet he was and of greet reverence –
He semed swich, his wordes weren so wise.
Justice he was ful often in assise,
315 By patente and by pleyn commissioun.
For his science and for his heigh renoun,
Of fees and robes hadde he many oon.
So greet a purchasour was nowher noon:
Al was fee symple to hym in effect;
320 His purchasyng myghte nat been infect.
Nowher so bisy a man as he ther nas,
And yet he semed bisier than he was.
In termes hadde he caas and doomes alle
That from the tyme of kyng William were falle.
325 Therto he koude endite and make a thyng,
Ther koude no wight pynche at his writyng;
And every statut koude he pleyn by rote.
He rood but hoomly in a medlee cote,
Girt with a ceint of silk, with barres smale;
330 Of his array telle I no lenger tale.
    A FRANKELEYN was in his compaignye.
Whit was his berd as is the dayesye;

Of his complexioun he was sangwyn.
Wel loved he by the morwe a sop in wyn;
335 To lyven in delit was evere his wone,
For he was Epicurus owene sone,
That heeld opinioun that pleyn delit
Was verray felicitee parfit.
An housholdere, and that a greet, was he;
340 Seint Julian he was in his contree.
His breed, his ale, was alweys after oon;
A bettre envyned man was nowher noon.
Withoute bake mete was nevere his hous,
Of fissh and flessh, and that so plentevous
345 It snewed in his hous of mete and drynke;
Of alle deyntees that men koude thynke,
After the sondry sesons of the yeer,
So chaunged he his mete and his soper.
Ful many a fat partrich hadde he in muwe,
350 And many a breem and many a luce in stuwe.
Wo was his cook but if his sauce were
Poynaunt and sharp, and redy al his geere.
His table dormant in his halle alway
Stood redy covered al the longe day.
355 At sessiouns ther was he lord and sire;
Ful ofte tyme he was knyght of the shire.
An anlaas and a gipser al of silk
Heeng at his girdel, whit as morne milk.
A shirreve hadde he been, and a contour.
360 Was nowher swich a worthy vavasour.

     An HABERDASSHERE and a CARPENTER,
A WEBBE, a DYERE, and a TAPYCER –
And they were clothed alle in o lyveree
Of a solempne and a greet fraternitee.
365 Ful fressh and newe hir geere apiked was;
Hir knyves were chaped noght with bras

But al with silver, wroght ful clene and weel,
Hire girdles and hir pouches everydeel.
Wel semed ech of hem a fair burgeys
370 To sitten in a yeldehalle on a deys.
Everich, for the wisdom that he kan,
Was shaply for to been an alderman.
For catel hadde they ynogh and rente,
And eek hir wyves wolde it wel assente;
375 And elles certeyn were they to blame.
It is ful fair to been ycleped 'madame',
And goon to vigilies al bifore,
And have a mantel roialliche ybore.

A COOK they hadde with hem for the nones
380 To boille the chiknes with the marybones,
And poudre-marchant tart and galyngale.
Wel koude he knowe a draughte of Londoun ale.
He koude rooste, and sethe, and broille, and frye,
Maken mortreux, and wel bake a pye.
385 But greet harm was it, as it thoughte me,
That on his shyne a mormal hadde he.
For blankmanger, that made he with the beste.

A SHIPMAN was ther, wonynge fer by weste;
For aught I woot, he was of Dertemouthe.
390 He rood upon a rouncy, as he kouthe,
In a gowne of faldyng to the knee.
A daggere hangynge on a laas hadde he
Aboute his nekke, under his arm adoun.
The hoote somer hadde maad his hewe al broun;
395 And certeinly he was a good felawe.
Ful many a draughte of wyn had he ydrawe
Fro Burdeux-ward, whil that the chapman sleep.
Of nyce conscience took he no keep.
If that he faught and hadde the hyer hond,
400 By water he sente hem hoom to every lond.

But of his craft to rekene wel his tydes,
His stremes, and his daungers hym bisides,
His herberwe, and his moone, his lodemenage,
Ther nas noon swich from Hulle to Cartage.
405 Hardy he was and wys to undertake;
With many a tempest hadde his berd been shake.
He knew alle the havenes, as they were,
Fro Gootlond to the cape of Fynystere,
And every cryke in Britaigne and in Spayne.
410 His barge ycleped was the Maudelayne.
　　　　With us ther was a DOCTOUR OF PHISIK;
In al this world ne was ther noon hym lik,
To speke of phisik and of surgerye,
For he was grounded in astronomye.
415 He kepte his pacient a ful greet deel
In houres by his magyk natureel.
Wel koude he fortunen the ascendent
Of his ymages for his pacient.
He knew the cause of everich maladye,
420 Were it of hoot, or coold, or moyste, or drye,
And where they engendred, and of what humour.
He was a verray, parfit praktisour:
The cause yknowe, and of his harm the roote,
Anon he yaf the sike man his boote.
425 Ful redy hadde he his apothecaries
To sende hym drogges and his letuaries,
For ech of hem made oother for to wynne –
Hir frendshipe nas nat newe to bigynne.
Wel knew he the olde Esculapius,
430 And Deyscorides, and eek Rufus,
Olde Ypocras, Haly, and Galyen,
Serapion, Razis, and Avycen,
Averrois, Damascien, and Constantyn,
Bernard, and Gatesden, and Gilbertyn.

435 Of his diete mesurable was he,
For it was of no superfluitee,
But of greet norissyng and digestible.
His studie was but litel on the Bible.
In sangwyn and in pers he clad was al,
440 Lyned with taffata and with sendal.
And yet he was but esy of dispence;
He kepte that he wan in pestilence.
For gold in phisik is a cordial,
Therefore he lovede gold in special.

445   A good WIF was ther OF biside BATHE,
But she was somdel deef, and that was scathe.
Of clooth-makyng she hadde swich an haunt
She passed hem of Ypres and of Gaunt.
In al the parisshe wif ne was ther noon
450 That to the offrynge bifore hire sholde goon;
And if ther dide, certeyn so wrooth was she
That she was out of alle charitee.
Hir coverchiefs ful fyne weren of ground;
I dorste swere they weyeden ten pound
455 That on a Sonday weren upon hir heed.
Hir hosen weren of fyn scarlet reed,
Ful streite yteyd, and shoes ful moyste and newe.
Boold was hir face, and fair, and reed of hewe.
She was a worthy womman al hir lyve:
460 Housbondes at chirche dore she hadde fyve,
Withouten oother compaignye in youthe –
But thereof nedeth nat to speke as nowthe.
And thries hadde she been at Jerusalem;
She hadde passed many a straunge strem;
465 At Rome she hadde been, and at Boloigne,
— In Galice at Seint-Jame, and at Coloigne.
She koude muchel of wandrynge by the weye.
Gat-tothed was she, soothly for to seye.

Upon an amblere esily she sat,
470 Ywympled wel, and on hir heed an hat
As brood as is a bokeler or a targe;
A foot-mantel aboute hir hipes large,
And on hir feet a paire of spores sharpe.
In felaweshipe wel koude she laughe and carpe.
475 Of remedies of love she knew per chaunce,
For she koude of that art the olde daunce.

   A good man was ther of religioun,
And was a povre PERSOUN OF A TOUN,
But riche he was of hooly thoght and werk.
480 He was also a lerned man, a clerk,
That Cristes gospel trewely wolde preche;
His parisshens devoutly wolde he teche.
Benygne he was, and wonder diligent,
And in adversitee ful pacient,
485 And swich he was ypreved ofte sithes.
Ful looth were hym to cursen for his tithes,
But rather wolde he yeven, out of doute,
Unto his povre parisshens aboute
Of his offryng and eek of his substaunce.
490 He koude in litel thyng have suffisaunce.
Wyd was his parisshe, and houses fer asonder,
But he ne lefte nat, for reyn ne thonder,
In siknesse nor in meschief to visite
The ferreste in his parisshe, muche and lite,
495 Upon his feet, and in his hand a staf.
This noble ensample to his sheep he yaf,
That first he wroghte, and afterward he taughte.
Out of the gospel he tho wordes caughte,
And this figure he added eek therto,
500 That if gold ruste, what shal iren do?
For if a preest be foul, on whom we truste,
No wonder is a lewed man to ruste;

And shame it is, if a prest take keep,
A shiten shepherde and a clene sheep.
505 Wel oghte a preest ensample for to yive,
By his clennesse, how that his sheep sholde lyve.
He sette nat his benefice to hyre
And leet his sheep encombred in the myre
And ran to Londoun unto Seinte Poules
510 To seken hym a chaunterie for soules,
Or with a bretherhed to been withholde;
But dwelte at hoom, and kepte wel his folde,
So that the wolf ne made it nat myscarie;
He was a shepherde and noght a mercenarie.
515 And though he hooly were and vertuous,
He was to synful men nat despitous,
Ne of his speche daungerous ne digne,
But in his techyng discreet and benygne.
To drawen folk to hevene by fairnesse,
520 By good ensample, this was his bisynesse.
But it were any persone obstinat,
What so he were, of heigh or lough estat,
Hym wolde he snybben sharply for the nonys.
A bettre preest I trowe that nowher noon ys.
525 He waited after no pompe and reverence,
Ne maked him a spiced conscience,
But Cristes loore and his apostles twelve
He taughte; but first he folwed it hymselve.
   With hym ther was a PLOWMAN, was his brother,
530 That hadde ylad of dong ful many a fother;
A trewe swynkere and a good was he,
Lyvynge in pees and parfit charitee.
God loved he best with al his hoole herte
At alle tymes, thogh him gamed or smerte,
535 And thanne his neighebor right as hymselve.
He wolde thresshe, and therto dyke and delve,

For Cristes sake, for every povre wight,
Withouten hire, if it lay in his myght.
His tithes payde he ful faire and wel,
540 Bothe of his propre swynk and his catel.
In a tabard he rood upon a mere.
      Ther was also a REVE, and a MILLERE,
A SOMNOUR, and a PARDONER also,
A MAUNCIPLE, and myself – ther were namo.
545   The MILLERE was a stout carl for the nones;
Ful byg he was of brawn, and eek of bones.
That proved wel, for over al ther he cam,
At wrastlynge he wolde have alwey the ram.
He was short-sholdred, brood, a thikke knarre;
550 Ther was no dore that he nolde heve of harre,
Or breke it at a rennyng with his heed.
His berd as any sowe or fox was reed,
And therto brood, as though it were a spade.
Upon the cop right of his nose he hade
555 A werte, and theron stood a toft of herys,
Reed as the brustles of a sowes erys;
His nosethirles blake were and wyde.
A swerd and a bokeler bar he by his syde.
His mouth as greet was as a greet forneys.
560 He was a janglere and a goliardeys,
And that was moost of synne and harlotries.
Wel koude he stelen corn and tollen thries;
And yet he hadde a thombe of gold, pardee.
A whit cote and a blew hood wered he.
565 A baggepipe wel koude he blowe and sowne,
And therwithal he broghte us out of towne.
      A gentil MAUNCIPLE was ther of a temple,
Of which achatours myghte take exemple
For to be wise in byynge of vitaille;
570 For wheither that he payde or took by taille,

Algate he wayted so in his achaat
That he was ay biforn and in good staat.
Now is nat that of God a ful fair grace
That swich a lewed mannes wit shal pace
575   The wisdom of an heep of lerned men?
Of maistres hadde he mo than thries ten,
That weren of lawe expert and curious,
Of which ther were a duszeyne in that hous
Worthy to been stywardes of rente and lond
580   Of any lord that is in Engelond,
To make hym lyve by his propre good
In honour dettelees (but if he were wood),
Or lyve as scarsly as hym list desire;
And able for to helpen al a shire
585   In any caas that myghte falle or happe.
And yet this Manciple sette hir aller cappe.
    The REVE was a sclendre colerik man.
His berd was shave as ny as ever he kan;
His heer was by his erys ful round yshorn;
590   His top was dokked lyk a preest biforn.
Ful longe were his legges and ful lene,
Ylyk a staf; ther was no calf ysene.
Wel koude he kepe a gerner and a bynne;
Ther was noon auditour koude on him wynne.
595   Wel wiste he by the droghte and by the reyn
The yeldynge of his seed and of his greyn.
His lordes sheep, his neet, his dayerye,
His swyn, his hors, his stoor, and his pultrye
Was hoolly in this Reves governynge,
600   And by his covenant yaf the rekenynge,
Syn that his lord was twenty yeer of age.
Ther koude no man brynge hym in arrerage.
Ther nas baillif, ne hierde, nor oother hyne,
That he ne knew his sleighte and his covyne;

605   They were adrad of hym as of the deeth.
      His wonyng was ful faire upon an heeth;
      With grene trees yshadwed was his place.
      He koude bettre than his lord purchace.
      Ful riche he was astored pryvely.
610   His lord wel koude he plesen subtilly,
      To yeve and lene hym of his owene good,
      And have a thank, and yet a cote and hood.
      In youthe he hadde lerned a good myster:
      He was a wel good wrighte, a carpenter.
615   This Reve sat upon a ful good stot
      That was al pomely grey and highte Scot.
      A long surcote of pers upon he hade,
      And by his syde he baar a rusty blade.
      Of Northfolk was this Reve of which I telle,
620   Biside a toun men clepen Baldeswelle.
      Tukked he was as is a frere aboute,
      And evere he rood the hyndreste of oure route.

          A SOMONOUR was ther with us in that place,
      That hadde a fyr-reed cherubynnes face,
625   For saucefleem he was, with eyen narwe.
      As hoot he was and lecherous as a sparwe,
      With scalled browes blake and piled berd.
      Of his visage children were aferd.
      Ther nas quyk-silver, lytarge, ne brymstoon,
630   Boras, ceruce, ne oille of tartre noon,
      Ne oynement that wolde clense and byte,
      That hym myghte helpen of his whelkes white,
      Nor of the knobbes sittynge on his chekes.
      Wel loved he garleek, oynons, and eek lekes,
635   And for to drynken strong wyn, reed as blood;
      Thanne wolde he speke and crie as he were wood.
      And whan that he wel dronken hadde the wyn,
      Thanne wolde he speke no word but Latyn.

A fewe termes hadde he, two or thre,
640 That he had lerned out of som decree –
No wonder is, he herde it al the day;
And eek ye knowen wel how that a jay
Kan clepen 'Watte' as wel as kan the pope.
But whoso koude in oother thyng hym grope,
645 Thanne hadde he spent al his philosophie;
Ay '*Questio quid iuris*' wolde he crie.
He was a gentil harlot and a kynde;
A bettre felawe sholde men noght fynde.
He wolde suffre for a quart of wyn
650 A good felawe to have his concubyn
A twelf month, and excuse hym atte fulle;
Ful prively a fynch eek koude he pulle.
And if he foond owher a good felawe,
He wolde techen him to have noon awe
655 In swich caas of the ercedekenes curs,
But if a mannes soule were in his purs;
For in his purs he sholde ypunysshed be.
'Purs is the ercedekenes helle,' seyde he.
But wel I woot he lyed right in dede;
660 Of cursyng oghte ech gilty man him drede,
For curs wol slee right as assoillyng savith,
And also war hym of a *Significavit*.
In daunger hadde he at his owene gise
The yonge girles of the diocise,
665 And knew hir conseil, and was al hir reed.
A gerland hadde he set upon his heed,
As greet as it were for an ale-stake.
A bokeleer hadde he maad hym of a cake.
    With hym ther rood a gentil PARDONER
670 Of Rouncivale, his freend and his compeer,
That streight was comen fro the court of Rome.
Ful loude he soong 'Com hider, love, to me!'

This Somonour bar to hym a stif burdoun;
Was nevere trompe of half so greet a soun.
675 This Pardoner hadde heer as yelow as wex,
But smothe it heeng as dooth a strike of flex;
By ounces henge his lokkes that he hadde,
And therwith he his shuldres overspradde;
But thynne it lay, by colpons oon and oon.
680 But hood, for jolitee, wered he noon,
For it was trussed up in his walet.
Hym thoughte he rood al of the newe jet;
Dischevelee, save his cappe, he rood al bare.
Swiche glarynge eyen hadde he as an hare.
685 A vernycle hadde he sowed upon his cappe.
His walet, biforn hym in his lappe,
Bretful of pardoun comen from Rome al hoot.
A voys he hadde as smal as hath a goot.
No berd hadde he, ne nevere sholde have;
690 As smothe it was as it were late shave.
I trowe he were a geldyng or a mare.
But of his craft, fro Berwyk into Ware
Ne was ther swich another pardoner.
For in his male he hadde a pilwe-beer,
695 Which that he seyde was Oure Lady veyl;
He seyde he hadde a gobet of the seyl
That Seint Peter hadde, whan that he wente
Upon the see, til Jhesu Crist hym hente.
He hadde a croys of latoun ful of stones,
700 And in a glas he hadde pigges bones.
But with thise relikes, whan that he fond
A povre person dwellynge upon lond,
Upon a day he gat hym moore moneye
Than that the person gat in monthes tweye;
705 And thus, with feyned flaterye and japes,
He made the person and the peple his apes.

But trewely to tellen atte laste,
He was in chirche a noble ecclesiaste.
Wel koude he rede a lessoun or a storie,
710 But alderbest he song an offertorie;
For wel he wiste, whan that song was songe,
He moste preche and wel affile his tonge
To wynne silver, as he ful wel koude;
Therefore he song the murierly and loude.

715   Now have I toold you soothly, in a clause,
Th'estaat, th'array, the nombre, and eek the cause
Why that assembled was this compaignye
In Southwerk at this gentil hostelrye
That highte the Tabard, faste by the Belle.
720 But now is tyme to yow for to telle
How that we baren us that ilke nyght,
Whan we were in that hostelrie alyght;
And after wol I telle of our viage
And al the remenaunt of oure pilgrimage.

725 But first I pray yow, of youre curteisye,
That ye n'arette it nat my vileynye,
Thogh that I pleynly speke in this mateere,
To telle yow hir wordes and hir cheere,
Ne thogh I speke hir wordes proprely.
730 For this ye knowen al so wel as I:
Whoso shal telle a tale after a man,
He moot reherce as ny as evere he kan
Everich a word, if it be in his charge,
Al speke he never so rudeliche and large,
735 Or ellis he moot telle his tale untrewe,
Or feyne thyng, or fynde wordes newe.
He may nat spare, althogh he were his brother;
He moot as wel seye o word as another.
Crist spak hymself ful brode in hooly writ,
740 And wel ye woot no vileynye is it.

Eek Plato seith, whoso kan hym rede,
The wordes moote be cosyn to the dede.
Also I prey yow to foryeve it me,
Al have I nat set folk in hir degree
745 Heere in this tale, as that they sholde stonde.
My wit is short, ye may wel understonde.
 Greet chiere made oure Hoost us everichon,
And to the soper sette he us anon.
He served us with vitaille at the beste;
750 Strong was the wyn, and wel to drynke us leste.
A semely man OURE HOOSTE was withalle
For to been a marchal in an halle.
A large man he was with eyen stepe –
A fairer burgeys was ther noon in Chepe –
755 Boold of his speche, and wys, and wel ytaught,
And of manhod hym lakkede right naught.
Eek therto he was right a myrie man;
And after soper pleyen he bigan,
And spak of myrthe amonges othere thynges,
760 Whan that we hadde maad oure rekenynges,
And seyde thus: 'Now, lordynges, trewely,
Ye been to me right welcome, hertely;
For by my trouthe, if that I shal nat lye,
I saugh nat this yeer so myrie a compaignye
765 Atones in this herberwe as is now.
Fayn wolde I doon yow myrthe, wiste I how.
And of a myrthe I am right now bythoght,
To doon yow ese, and it shal coste noght.
 'Ye goon to Caunterbury – God yow speede,
770 The blisful martir quite yow youre meede!
And wel I woot, as ye goon by the weye,
Ye shapen yow to talen and to pleye;
For trewely, confort ne myrthe is noon
To ride by the weye doumb as a stoon;

775   And therfore wol I maken yow disport,
      As I seyde erst, and doon yow som confort.
      And if yow liketh alle by oon assent
      For to stonden at my juggement,
      And for to werken as I shal yow seye,
780   Tomorwe, whan ye riden by the weye,
      Now, by my fader soule that is deed,
      But ye be myrie, I wol yeve yow myn heed!
      Hoold up youre hondes, withouten moore speche.'
        Oure conseil was nat longe for to seche.
785   Us thoughte it was noght worth to make it wys,
      And graunted hym withouten moore avys,
      And bad him seye his voirdit as hym leste.
      'Lordynges,' quod he, 'now herkneth for the beste;
      But taak it nought, I prey yow, in desdeyn.
790   This is the poynt, to speken short and pleyn,
      That ech of yow, to shorte with oure weye,
      In this viage shal telle tales tweye
      To Caunterbury-ward, I mene it so,
      And homward he shal tellen othere two,
795   Of aventures that whilom han bifalle.
      And which of yow that bereth hym best of alle –
      That is to seyn, that telleth in this caas
      Tales of best sentence and moost solaas –
      Shal have a soper at oure aller cost
800   Heere in this place, sittynge by this post,
      Whan that we come agayn fro Caunterbury.
      And for to make yow the moore mury,
      I wol myselven goodly with yow ryde,
      Right at myn owene cost, and be youre gyde;
805   And whoso wole my juggement withseye
      Shal paye al that we spenden by the weye.
      And if ye vouche sauf that it be so,
      Tel me anon, withouten wordes mo,

And I wol erly shape me therfore.'
810   This thyng was graunted, and oure othes swore
With ful glad herte, and preyden hym also
That he wolde vouche sauf for to do so,
And that he wolde been oure governour,
And of oure tales juge and reportour,
815   And sette a soper at a certeyn pris,
And we wol reuled been at his devys
In heigh and lough; and thus by oon assent
We been acorded to his juggement.
And therupon the wyn was fet anon;
820   We dronken, and to reste wente echon,
Withouten any lenger taryynge.
      Amorwe, whan that day bigan to sprynge,
Up roos oure Hoost, and was oure aller cok,
And gadrede us togidre alle in a flok,
825   And forth we riden a litel moore than paas
Unto the Wateryng of Seint Thomas;
And there oure Hoost bigan his hors areste
And seyde, 'Lordynges, herkneth, if yow leste.
Ye woot youre foreward, and I it yow recorde.
830   If even-song and morwe-song accorde,
Lat se now who shal telle the firste tale.
As evere mote I drynke wyn or ale,
Whoso be rebel to my juggement
Shal paye for al that by the wey is spent.
835   Now draweth cut, er that we ferrer twynne;
He which that hath the shorteste shal bigynne.
Sire Knyght,' quod he, 'my mayster and my lord,
Now draweth cut, for that is myn accord.
Cometh neer,' quod he, 'my lady Prioresse.
840   And ye, sire Clerk, lat be youre shamefastnesse,
Ne studieth noght; ley hond to, every man!'
Anon to drawen every wight bigan,

And shortly for to tellen as it was,
Were it by aventure, or sort, or cas,
845 The sothe is this: the cut fil to the Knyght,
Of which ful blithe and glad was every wyght,
And telle he moste his tale, as was resoun,
By foreward and by composicioun,
As ye han herd; what nedeth wordes mo?
850 And whan this goode man saugh that it was so,
As he that wys was and obedient
To kepe his foreward by his free assent,
He seyde, 'Syn I shal bigynne the game,
What, welcome be the cut, a Goddes name!
855 Now lat us ryde, and herkneth what I seye.'
And with that word we ryden forth oure weye,
And he bigan with right a myrie cheere
His tale anon, and seyde as ye may heere.

Notes

The Canterbury Tales is a collection of stories told by a group of narrators. This was a familiar way of organizing a book in the late fourteenth century. For example, Boccaccio's Italian prose work the *Decameron*, composed between 1348 and 1353, relates the hundred stories told by ten young people of noble birth during the ten days they stayed at a villa outside Florence in order to escape the plague of 1348. But Chaucer is original in his choice of setting, a pilgrimage – a journey to Canterbury to pray at the shrine of St Thomas à Becket. Such collections of stories normally began by describing the circumstances in which the storytellers came together, but Chaucer adds elaborate portrayals of each pilgrim. By describing so many people he offers a portrait of the society in which he lived, in the tradition of medieval estates satire. (See Interpretations, page 91 and Jill Mann, *Chaucer and Medieval Estates Satire*.)

The *General Prologue* begins by describing the season and Chaucer's meeting with the other pilgrims, continues with the individual descriptions of them, and concludes by setting out the terms of the competition in which the tales are to be told. Throughout the *General Prologue* the reader is invited to ask questions, to see implications and to evaluate the reliability and perceptiveness of the narrator figure, one of the pilgrims who is called 'Chaucer', but who seems to be more naive and less skilled than the author of *The Canterbury Tales*. (See Interpretations, pages 101–105.)

Another issue which it is best to raise at the outset, since you will be involved with it throughout, is Chaucer's use of irony. Irony is saying one thing and meaning another. Typically someone might use words which praise in order to condemn. For example someone might say 'well done', when I spill the tea on the floor. In normal conversation we might call this sarcasm, and recognize it as a form of verbal abuse which is especially

enjoyable for onlookers and especially wounding for the victim.
Writers often use irony to amuse audiences and to attack people
or practices. The difficulty is to decide from a written text when
a term of praise is meant seriously and when it is meant
ironically. In conversation we can usually tell from the tone of
voice employed. In reading a text we have to look for evidence of
a mismatch between the language employed and the view
presented. So that whether or not a particular expression is taken
as ironic may depend on a person's own opinion about one of
the pilgrims. Some people think that the words of praise which
Chaucer applies to the Knight are intended ironically, others take
them at face value. Sometimes new historical discoveries can
alter our judgements of irony. For example, people used to think
that it was an affectation for the Prioress to sing mass through
her nose (122–3). This made them read many of the positive
words applied to her as ironic. Putting these ironies alongside her
other shortcomings, they regarded the whole portrait as a bitter
denunciation. In the 1940s it was discovered that some medieval
books recommend a nasal delivery in order to rest the voice. This
weakened the case for interpreting Chaucer's words ironically
and opened the possibility of a more positive reading of the
Prioress.

The opening: Lines 1–18

Long poems often begin with long sentences, as if to proclaim
the poet's skill at the outset. In his opening sentence Chaucer
brings together many different ideas and sensations within a
structure which remains clear and unforced. The sentence seems
to move through four phases. It begins with nature: the rain
water making the earth fruitful, and the air breathing life into the
fields, as if the world is being created anew. Then it turns to
generation, with the growth of the plants in spring and the
courtship songs and matings of the birds. Next it speaks of

humans who are moved to travel great distances on pilgrimage in the spring, because the roads are now passable, and because spring rekindles the love of God, as much as earthly love. Finally the focus narrows to England, where people travel particularly to the shrine of St Thomas, renowned for its miracles of healing. Do you think that this sentence reconciles these natural, human and supernatural aspects of spring? Or are there tensions between, say, the awakening of sexual love and the religious urge to go on pilgrimages? Can you think of other tensions in the sentence?

This sentence is full of realistic detail (the April showers [1], the plants [4], the birds [9], the pilgrims [12]) as if Chaucer were writing the literary equivalent of the paintings of 'labours of the months' in medieval books of hours. (See the illustration for April on page 100.) But critics have also pointed to the way in which it exploits literary tradition, particularly the tradition of the springtime opening of the medieval dream-vision. Compare this passage with those printed in the Appendix (pages 181–182). (See also Interpretations, pages 99–101.)

2 **droghte of March** Is March usually a dry month in Britain? Or is this a literary convention (based perhaps on poems written in Italy or Greece)?

2–3 **to the roote... every veyne** literally the roots and veins belong to plants which will produce the flowers (4). Grammatically they also belong to the drought and by association to the earth.

3–4 **swich licour... flour** liquid by whose power the flower is brought into being. The sense is that the rising of the sap promotes new growth and initiates the reproductive cycle of the plant.

5 **Zephirus** the mild west wind, envisaged in classical mythology as a god.

6 **Inspired** breathed life into.

7 **croppes** shoots.

8 **Ram... yronne** a much debated problem, though not a very important one. Prior to the reform of the calendar (1582 in

most Catholic countries, 1752 in Britain) the sun was in Aries (*the Ram*) roughly between 11 March and 11 April. Halfway through Aries would therefore be about 25 March, which would contradict line 1. So Walter Skeat in his 1890 edition of *The Canterbury Tales* suggests that the sun had completed the *second* half of Aries, which brings the date to 11 or 12 April. This would fit in reasonably well with 16 or 17 April, the dates implied for *The Parson's Tale*, which is delivered a few days after Chaucer meets the pilgrims. But both these dates are difficult to reconcile with 18 April, mentioned as the date of *The Sergeant of the Law's Tale*. Perhaps Chaucer would have sorted out this confusion if he had lived to revise the whole poem for publication. The sun is *yonge* (7) because Aries is the first sign of the solar new year, beginning at the spring equinox.

10 **open ye**   Chaucer may be alluding to the belief that the nightingale sings continuously for fifteen days in the mating season. (See also line 98.)

11 **So... corages**   so nature spurs them in their desires. Literally *corage* means 'heart' or 'spirit', but it often carries a sexual connotation. Could there be something ironic or subversive about Chaucer's decision to rhyme *corages* with *pilgrimages* (12)?

13 **palmeres**   pilgrims who carried a palm leaf as a sign that they had visited the Holy Land.
straunge strondes   foreign shores.

17 **blisful martir**   blessed martyr, St Thomas à Becket, Archbishop of Canterbury, who was murdered by followers of Henry II in his cathedral on 29 December 1170. Becket's shrine had a reputation for miraculous healing. Hence it was much visited and richly decorated with gold and jewels. The idea here is that the pilgrims are visiting the shrine not to be healed, but to give thanks to the saint for his intercession in helping them overcome sickness in the past.

The scene at the Tabard: Lines 19–42

Where the first sentence evokes the large context of spring and pilgrimage, the second brings us firmly down to local reality, with Chaucer taking a night's lodging at a real and rather well-appointed inn, the Tabard in Southwark. Southwark at this time was a small town at the south end of London Bridge, outside the jurisdiction of the city of London. Pilgrims often lodged in Southwark prior to setting out on the road to Canterbury. It was quite usual for travellers to band together for protection against the dangers of the road.

Chaucer sets the pilgrimage story in motion and then immediately suspends it in order to describe his fellow pilgrims.

What is your first impression of Chaucer, the narrator of the poem? (See Interpretations, pages 101–105.)

19–26 This sentence is analysed in A Note on Chaucer's English, p. 154.

22 **with ful devout corage** in a very pious spirit.

24 **nyne and twenty** the *General Prologue* mentions 30 pilgrims (including the three priests who accompany the Prioress, but excluding Chaucer and the innkeeper, Harry Baily). Perhaps Chaucer intended 29 so that when he joined he would bring the number in the story-telling competition to 30, or perhaps he miscounted.

29 **And... beste** And we were certainly made very comfortable.

33 **forward** agreement.

37 **Me... resoun** It seems to me logical.

38–41 Chaucer here indicates that he will describe the circumstances (*condicioun* [38]), occupation (*whiche they weren* [40]), social rank (*degree* [40]) and dress (*array* [41]) of the pilgrims. How far do Chaucer's descriptions fit in with the pattern he offers here?

42 Many different theories have been advanced about the order of the portraits. Jill Mann in her book, *Chaucer and Medieval Estates Satire* points out that Chaucer avoids the usual order of Medieval Estates Satire (first clergy, then laity, then

women). Michael Alexander in *Prologue to The Canterbury Tales* (p. 54) suggests the following scheme:

1	Military	Knight, Squire, Yeoman
2	Clergy	Prioress, Monk, Friar
3	Bourgeois	Merchant, Clerk, Sergeant of the Law, Franklin, Five Guildsmen, Cook, Shipman, Doctor of Physic, Wife of Bath
4	Good men	Parson, Ploughman
5	Petty Bourgeois	Miller, Manciple, Reeve
6	Church Officers	Summoner, Pardoner

Can you point out any inconsistencies in this scheme? (It may not be easy to think of a better one.) Perhaps the order is pragmatic, as though Chaucer started by placing together people who are related (as individuals or as a social group). When this became predictable, he varied it by putting contrasting characters together. Sometimes he uses the ordering to point out similarities we might not have suspected.

The Knight: Lines 43–78

Knights were soldiers who fought on horseback. They held lands in return for military service to their feudal overlords, the barons. In the feudal system, the King theoretically owned all the land in his realm. He granted control over large tracts of land to the great lords of the realm in return for service, financial and military, and loyalty. The great lords granted lands to lesser lords on similar terms. In the same way the lesser lords granted lands to the knights. This meant, firstly, that everyone apart from the king owed service to a superior, and secondly, that a well organized army could be raised from the land when it was required. Knights rented part of their lands out to farmers in return for produce or services. Local inhabitants, both freemen and serfs, were obliged to devote part of their time to working on the knight's estate. Peasant farmers only held land from him as tenants and he was responsible for the administration of law within his territory. Usually the eldest son of a knight would inherit all his father's lands, leaving the younger sons with the necessity of making their own way economically, through marriage (in that the bride's father would give property to the couple) or through service to their elder brother or another feudal lord. Chaucer's description of the Knight makes no reference to his lands (though perhaps the presence of the Yeoman indicates that he had some) or to his administrative responsibilities. Perhaps he neglected them or perhaps he was a younger son.

Chaucer describes the Knight's values, his campaigns, his behaviour and his appearance. Other aspects of knightly life (love, hunting) appear in the portraits of the Squire and the Yeoman. Do the many approving adjectives (e.g. *worthy* used five times) support the traditional view that the Knight is an ideal figure beside whom the others can be judged, or should we take them ironically? Whereas most English soldiers of his time would have fought in France, the Knight's campaigns in Spain, Morocco, Turkey and the Baltic states were all crusades. Terry Jones in *Chaucer's Knight* has suggested that these particular campaigns were disreputable and that Chaucer meant us to regard the Knight as a mercenary. Maurice Keen ('Chaucer's Knight, the English Aristocracy and the Crusade'), in reply, pointed to evidence of the prestige of crusading among late-fourteenth-century English aristocrats. Some of them took part for religious reasons, others for personal glory, but fighting in France was more lucrative. What do you think Chaucer tells us about the Knight's motives? What is the significance of his plain, rust-stained clothes?

45–6 These five qualities summarize the ideals of knightly behaviour: skill in fighting (*chivalrie*), loyalty and honesty (*trouthe*), honourable behaviour, generosity (*fredom*), and good manners and consideration for others (*curteisie*). (See Interpretations, pages 107–110.)

47 Probably the reference is to the Knight's feudal overlord, but it could mean God, in which case *therto* (48) would mean 'for that purpose'.

48 **therto**   in addition.
   ferre   farther.

49 **hethenesse**   non-Christian countries.

51–67 The places and the battles Chaucer mentions fall into four groups. Algeciras (*Algezir* [57]) in the kingdom of Granada (*Gernade* [56]), part of Spain, was captured from the Muslims in 1344. A raid on Morocco (*Belmarye* [57]) may have been connected with this campaign. King Peter of Cyprus led campaigns against the Muslims in the near East. He attacked Antalya (*Satalye* [58]) in Turkey in 1361, Alexandria (*Alisaundre* [51]) in Egypt in 1365 and Ayash (*Lyeys* [58]) in modern Lebanon in 1367. The independent Muslim prince of Balat (*Palatye* [65]) in Turkey made peace with Peter in 1365. The Teutonic knights (a religious order of German knights and priests, founded in 1189) made raids (*reysed* [54]) from Prussia (*Pruce* [53]) into Lithuania (*Lettow* [54]) and Russia (*Ruce* [54]) throughout the second half of the fourteenth century. They aimed to settle parts of the modern Baltic republics under Christian control. There is no record of a Christian attack on Tlemcen (*Tramyssene* [62]) in Algeria in the fourteenth century. Terry Jones (*Chaucer's Knight*) suggests that the Knight fought for a Muslim prince there. Do you think that the context (*for oure feith* [62]) will allow this? Jill Mann (*Chaucer and Medieval Estates Satire*) says that lists of campaigns often appear in courtly descriptions, to demonstrate the worth of a knight and to evoke the romance of distant countries. What should we make of the disorder of this list of campaigns?

52 He had sat in the place of honour at the head of the table. The Teutonic knights sometimes held feasts to honour the deeds of knights who had come to their aid.

54 **reysed**   ridden on raids.

59 **Grete See**   Mediterranean Sea.

63 **lystes**   literally the arena erected for a tournament, here 'formal duels', presumably fought by representatives from the opposing armies.

67 **everemoore** always.
   sovereyn prys pre-eminent reputation.
69 **port** behaviour, manner.
   meeke humble, submissive. Is the Knight's exceptionally modest behaviour and speech a sign of virtue, or is it difficult to believe?
70 **vileynye** rude words, vulgarity. Literally the language (or the behaviour) appropriate to a *villein*, someone low born. In Middle English words connected with high birth (*gentil, fre*) are associated with virtuous and admirable behaviour, while words denoting low birth acquire negative meanings. How much does this linguistic bias in favour of the well born continue into modern English? (Consider the use of words like 'noble' or 'common'.)
71 **no maner wight** any sort of person.
72 **verray** true.
   parfit perfect.
   gentil noble, gracious. Are we to think that this comment is justified? Is it meant ironically? Or is the naïve approval of Chaucer the pilgrim undercut by the factual detail of the portrait?
74 **gay** richly clothed.
75 **fustian** coarse cloth.
   gypon tunic.
76 Stained (with rust) from his coat of chain-mail (*habergeon*).

The Squire: Lines 79–100

A squire was a young male member of the knightly class who was preparing to become a knight, learning the customs of his order by serving an established knight. Chaucer's Squire performs the relatively menial task of carving his father's meat. His fighting experience is different from his father's and so are his interests. The Squire has many of the accomplishments expected of a young courtier and some aspects of the description (and the language in which it is couched) are conventional. Some critics have found the Squire's devotion to love excessive while others have praised him for his youthful vitality and his artistic inclinations. What do you think the contrasts between father and son mean?

80 **lusty**   lively.
   bacheler   bachelor; the degree of knighthood which the Squire has attained rather than 'unmarried man'. (Compare with Bachelor of Arts.)
81 **crulle**   curled.
   presse   press, curler.
83 **evene lengthe**   moderate height.
84 **delyvere**   active, agile.
85 **somtyme**   once.
   in chyvachie   on a cavalry expedition.
86 Flanders, Artois and Picardy are districts of northern France (now partly in Belgium) where Chaucer himself served in the army in his youth.
87 **born hym**   conducted himself.
   space   time.
88 **stonden in his lady grace**   win the favour of his lady. The Squire goes to war to show off his skill and impress his lady.
89 **Embrouded**   (his clothes were) embroidered.
   meede   meadow.
91 **floytynge**   playing the flute.
92 **fressh**   youthful, blooming, vigorous.
93 Should we admire the Squire's elegant, fashionable clothes, or is some criticism intended? See the illustration of the Squire from the Ellesmere manuscript on page 109.
94–6 Knights were expected to be skilful riders. Dancing, writing music and poetry, and jousting were considered suitable accomplishments for aristocratic young men. *Purtreye* (96) may mean 'describe' rather than 'draw' because courtiers were not usually taught drawing.
97 **by nyghtertale**   at night time. (See line 10.)
99 **lowely**   modest.
   servysable   attentive, willing to serve. It is to the Squire's credit that he serves his father willingly and gracefully.

The Yeoman: Lines 101–117

A yeoman was a free servant (i.e. not a serf as many of the agricultural workers were), above the grooms but below the squire in a feudal household. By profession the Yeoman is a forester, a gamekeeper, but here he serves as the Knight's bodyguard. (See lines 111–14.) There was no tradition of describing foresters in estates satire. Chaucer concentrates on the Yeoman's appearance and the tools of his trade.

101 **namo**   no more. Why does the Knight (*he*) not have a larger retinue?

102 **hym liste**   he preferred to.

104 Peacock feathers were (and are) used in making good quality arrows.

    kene   sharp.

105 **bar ful thriftily**   carried very carefully.

106 **dresse**   care for, prepare.

    takel   tackle, equipment.

    yemanly   skilfully, as a yeoman should.

107 Feathers which did not stand out properly (*fetheres lowe*) would cause an arrow to fall short (*droupe*).

109 **not heed**   a close-cropped head. The Yeoman's face is brown (*broun*) from exposure to sun, wind and rain.

110 He understood all the customs and practices of woodcraft. In this period woodcraft may refer particularly to gamekeeping and hunting.

111 **gay bracer**   bright armguard.

112 **bokeler**   small shield.

114 **Harneised**   mounted, ornamented.

115 **Cristopher**   a medallion of St Christopher, patron saint of travellers.

    sheene   bright.

116 **bawdryk**   baldric, shoulderstrap. What is the effect of the portrait of the Yeoman? Does Chaucer include it to amplify

his portrayal of the Knight, to remind us that commoners
fought alongside nobles, or to extend his picture of the
activities of the land?

The Prioress: Lines 118–164

The Prioress, first of the group of ecclesiastical figures, is one of
only two women described in the *General Prologue* (the Wife of
Bath is the other). What might this imply? The interpretation of
the portrait has been much fought over in relation to debates
about the nature of Chaucer's irony.

Two fundamental points seem to be agreed: that the external
details of the portrait (her name [121], her table manners [127–36],
her social behaviour [137–41] and her appearance [151–4, 157–62])
imitate the descriptions of heroines in romances and that many of
her actions are unsuited to a nun. For example, nuns were
forbidden to go on pilgrimages, to keep dogs and to wear
fashionable clothes. There are also faults of omission. One might
expect that the description of a nun would say more about her
religious life and about her concern for the sufferings of other
humans. Some critics (such as James Winny, in his Cambridge
edition of the *General Prologue*) see Chaucer's underlying purpose
as satirical, to expose the gulf between her charming and
complacent social exterior and the true obligations of her calling.
But there are other ways of interpreting the difference between
Chaucer's portrait and our expectations about nuns. For E.T.
Donaldson (*Chaucer's Poetry*), Chaucer the pilgrim is so
overwhelmed by the charm of the Prioress that his naïve and
inappropriate praise reveals his infatuation more than it establishes
her excellence. Derek Pearsall (*The Canterbury Tales*), on the other
hand, insists that the mildness of the Prioress's failings forces the
reader to 'feel that his urge to disapprove is unduly harsh'. For him
the portrait makes a strict moral judgement of the Prioress
impossible. Jill Mann (*Chaucer and Medieval Estates Satire*) has

shown that some medieval writers identified a spiritual courtliness appropriate to the nun as the beloved of Christ, though she concludes that the Prioress's *curteisie* (132) is wordly rather than spiritual. We should also remember that although the *General Prologue* says nothing about her religious convictions, the prologue to her tale is a prayer. The tale itself combines a simple Christian piety with a streak of violent anti-semitism.

The portrait also raises questions about the relationship between literature and historical reality. The expenses involved in arranging marriages at the higher social levels meant that many younger daughters of noble families found themselves in the Prioress's position, caught between two codes. Brought up in a courtly atmosphere, they could find themselves at the age of 15 or 16 forced into a religious life for which they felt little real vocation. Eileen Power, in a chapter on Madame Eglentyne in her pioneering social history, *Medieval People*, has shown that many of the Prioress's failings reflect the reality of fourteenth-century convent life as revealed in visitation records (records of the regular inspections of monasteries and convents carried out by the local bishop). Power quotes a Lincoln visitation of 1436 in which the nuns complain that their prioress wears:

> golden rings exceeding costly, with divers precious stones and also girdles silvered and gilded over and silken veils and she carries her veil too high above her forehead, so that her forehead, being entirely uncovered, can be seen of all, and she wears furs of vair [a type of squirrel]. Also she wears shifts of cloth of Rennes, which costs sixteen pence the ell [about 115 cm]. Also she wears kirtles laced with silk and tiring pins of silver and silver gilt and has made all the nuns wear the like... Item she has on her neck a long silken band, in English a lace, which hangs down below her breast and thereon a golden ring with one diamond. (p. 85)

119 **symple and coy** innocent and quiet. These two adjectives are often found together in descriptions of courtly heroines. *Coy* implies shyness but not coquettishness. How do you

think we should interpret Chaucer's decision to begin his description of a nun by talking about her smile?

120 **ooth** strictly speaking a prioress should neither swear nor go on pilgrimages, but if her strongest oath is such a mild one it is unlikely that much criticism is intended.

Seinte Loy St Eligius (588–629), by trade a goldsmith. He was renowned for his beauty and courtliness.

122 **Eglentyne** literally 'briar rose' but also a name found in romances. Nuns choose a new name when they make their vows. Would you draw conclusions from the Prioress's choice of this name rather than one associated with a virtue or a religious figure? (See Interpretations, page 134.)

123 Intoned with nasal delivery very elegantly. The possible ironies of language are very carefully balanced. *Ful semely* (123) and *ful weel* (122) could be ironic, but since they describe her skill in singing the mass they might well be meant seriously. Nasal delivery was not an affectation but a way of taking strain off the voice. What do you make of Chaucer's rather frequent use of the intensifier *ful* (very) in this passage?

124–6 Speaking French was an important courtly skill. Even though French was no longer the language of government (as it had been from the Norman Conquest until the early fourteenth century) it was still the language of culture and law. English poets of the time, such as Chaucer's friend John Gower, wrote in French and Latin as well as in English.

Some scholars take the Prioress's very elegant (*ful faire and fetisly* [124]) French literally, arguing that the nuns at St Leonard's convent in Stratford at Bow spoke a good version of Anglo-Norman French, as opposed to the Parisian French spoken at court and at a nearby convent at Barking. Others assume that the phrase is ironic and that Chaucer is making a joke about her Essex French. Which view seems more likely to you? Would Chaucer's position be inconsistent if he was criticizing the Prioress's over-courtly manners (127–41) at the same time as looking down on the quality of her French?

129–31 Forks were not in common use in England until the sixteenth century, so polite eating required a certain manual dexterity (as it still does in some countries). Do Chaucer's remarks suggest that the Prioress was excessively interested in the etiquette of eating, or merely that she had mastered an important skill? Why does he not talk about the table manners of other pilgrims? There is also a literary joke here. Chaucer is translating directly from a passage in the Old French poem the *Roman de la Rose* (c. 1275) in which La Vieille advises a young woman about how to attract men. (See Interpretations, page 135 and Appendix, pages 182–3).

132   She took the greatest pleasure in good manners.

133   **over-lippe**   upper lip.

134   **ferthyng**   drop, literally a farthing, a small round coin worth a quarter of an old penny.

136   'She reached for her food very graciously.' What is the effect of using so many words which indicate approval (*wel, ful semely, ful plesaunt*)?

137   **of greet desport**   very merry.

138   **amyable of port**   friendly in her manner.

139–40   **countrefete cheere/Of court**   to imitate the behaviour of the court.

141   **to ben holden digne**   to be considered worthy.

142–5   What do you think it means that Chaucer speaks of her *conscience* and her feelings of charity and pity in relation to a mouse caught in a trap rather than in relation to other cases which might require compassion? Compare the use of *conscience* and *tendre herte* in line 150.

147   **wastel-breed**   the most expensive bread generally available. Meat was usually too expensive to feed to dogs. What is Chaucer saying when he suggests that the Prioress's dogs ate better than most people? Eileen Power, in her book *Medieval People*, quotes a Winchester visitation of 1387 which complains about the animals (birds, hounds and rabbits) which the nuns bring into church with them, noting that the hunting dogs in the convent were eating the food which ought to be given to the poor, and fouling the cloisters.

150   **conscience**   solicitude, pity.

151   **wympul**   wimple, garment covering the whole head apart from the face (like a balaclava).
      pynched   pleated.

152–6   The well-formed (*tretys*) nose, the grey eyes and the small mouth were typical of the romance heroine, as was this type of part-by-part description (sometimes called a 'blazon'). But the Prioress's forehead may be too wide (though a certain breadth was a sign of beauty) and *she was nat undergrowe* may well be an understatement to indicate that she was very large. Might these lines explain why she became a nun rather than a nobleman's wife?

158–9 A nun ought to carry a rosary (a string of beads used to remember a sequence of prayers), but should it be as colourful as this one? The *gauds*, large beads representing *The Lord's Prayer*, are placed after every ten of the smaller beads, each of which represents *Hail Mary*, a shorter prayer addressed to St Mary, mother of Jesus Christ.

160–1 Nuns were not supposed to wear brooches. A crowned 'A' was a contemporary symbol for Queen Anne, wife of Richard II. How might these 'facts' influence your interpretation of Chaucer's view of the Prioress? What meaning does Chaucer convey by making the brooch hang from (*theron*) the rosary?

162 **Amor vincit omnia**   (Latin) Love conquers all things. Do you think this refers to human love (appropriate to the would-be heroine of a romance) or to love of God (appropriate to the nun)? John Livingston Lowes comments in *Convention and Revolt in Poetry*, 'Which of the two loves does "Amor" mean to the Prioress? I do not know; but I think she thought she meant love celestial.'

163 The presence of a secretary (*chapeleyne* [164]) and three priests confirms the high status of the Prioress.

The Monk: Lines 165–207

Monks made vows to remove themselves from the world and devote themselves to prayer and contemplation. They lived in regulated communities, monasteries, which were usually situated at a distance from towns, or in remote places. Monasteries were often centres of religious devotion, learning and culture, but when they became wealthy, through agriculture or the gifts of local people, they could offer a life of easy self-indulgence. The long history of Christian monasticism (from the fourth century AD to the present) is marked by successive waves of reform, attempts to renew the ideal of selfless devotion to prayer.

Chaucer's Monk loves hunting, good food and fine clothes. (See Interpretations, pages 119–120.) He regards the rules of his order as old-fashioned and rather strict (174). Some critics think that Chaucer's attitude to the Monk is basically friendly, his satire gentle at most, where others treat the apparent approval (183) as bitterly ironic. Some recent critics detect the Monk's own voice in the amusing replies to those who criticize monks for breaking the rules. Jill Mann (*Chaucer and Medieval Estates Satire*) shows that Chaucer's description of the Monk's failings reflects traditions of anti-clerical satire. She argues that Chaucer omits the moral condemnation which would be usual in his sources. Must it be wrong for a monk to devote so much time to hunting and eating well? Or is he a charming man whose vices harm no one but himself?

165 **a... maistrie** a good one, surpassing the others.
166 **outridere** a monk with business outside the monastery (most monks were confined within the monastery walls).
    venerie hunting (sometimes used in the sense of pursuing love).
167 Does Chaucer mean that the Monk is worldly (or sexually active?) and seeking to become head of his monastery, or merely that he is companionable and may go far? Would this Monk really make a good abbot, or does he just think he would? Or is Chaucer implying that abbots are often as worldly as his Monk?
171 What effect does Chaucer achieve by comparing the jingling of the bells on his bridle to the sound of a chapel bell?
172 The Monk is in charge (*kepere*) of a small house (*celle*) of monks separate from the main monastery. Does Chaucer call him a lord because he remembers that monks often have the title *Dom* (short for *dominus* (Latin) meaning 'lord') or because he wants to convey something about this Monk's manner?
173 St Benedict (*Beneit*), c.480–c.547, drew up a rule which established Christian monasticism in Western Europe. His

disciple St Maurus (*Maure*) is said to have brought the rule to France. What is Chaucer's attitude to the Monk's dismissal of the rule in the next few lines?

176 And followed the fashion of the modern world.

177 **pulled** plucked. A plucked hen and an oyster were both of little value, but they suggest that the Monk measures things according to his love of food. Scholars argue about which *text* Chaucer refers to here.

179 **recchelees** careless (about keeping the rules).

183 Does Chaucer agree with the Monk, or is his apparent approval an ironic way of highlighting the outrageousness of what the Monk says?

184–7 Monks were supposed to study and work (*swynken* [186]) with their hands.

187 **Austyn** St Augustine of Hippo, 354–430, one of the greatest bishops and writers (e.g. *Confessions, City of God, On Christian Doctrine*) of the early Christian Church, was reputed to have written a monastic rule.

bit commands. Should the Monk be concerned with serving the world? Is Chaucer agreeing that observing the rule is futile, or are we here hearing the complacent voice of the Monk himself? Might this be a place where we should distinguish the approval of Chaucer the pilgrim from the irony of Chaucer the poet?

189 **prikasour** horseman, hunter. Why *Therfore?*

191 **prikyng** tracking (perhaps with a sexual·innuendo).

193 His sleeves are lined (*purfiled*) at the wrist with the expensive fur (*grys* [194]) of the squirrel.

196 **curious** skilfully made.

197 **love-knotte** a knot or bow-shaped decoration.
gretter larger.
Love-knotte might describe only the shape of the pin, or it might indicate its significance. Monks should not have expensive ornaments or (still less) love-tokens.

200 **poynt** condition.

201 **stepe** prominent.

202 'Gleamed like a fire under a cauldron.' Does Chaucer admire the Monk's physique and his twinkling eyes, or is he criticizing his overindulgence in food and drink?

203 **greet estaat**   fine condition.
204 **prelaat**   prelate, high-ranking churchman.
205 **forpyned goost**   tormented spirit.
206 Roast swan was very expensive. James Winny in his
   Cambridge edition of *The General Prologue* (p. 96) suggests
   that while the Monk was a complete failure in his profession,
   Chaucer admired his vitality and his joyful response to life.
   Do you agree? How is the sense of the Monk's vitality
   conveyed?

The Friar: Lines 208–269

The orders of friars were founded in the early thirteenth
century by St Dominic, 1170–1221, and St Francis of Assisi,
1181–1226. Friars tended to be well-educated (many of the most
famous theologians and philosophers of the thirteenth and
fourteenth centuries were friars) and friaries were established in
towns and near universities. Individual friars were supposed to
have no possessions and to live by begging from the people they
served (hence they were called mendicants), but friaries soon
became rich from the gifts of wealthy people. The most splendid
churches in most Italian cities belong to the Franciscans and the
Dominicans. The parish clergy, who tended to lose out in the
competition for gifts and legacies, often accused the friars of
cultivating the rich and giving them easy penances. Estates Satire
echoes these complaints.

   Chaucer emphasizes his Friar's smooth talk, his involvement
with women, his fine dress and the profits he makes from the abuse
of confession (218–32). These characteristics conflict with his
vows of poverty, chastity and obedience, but he is not the
avaricious lecher sometimes found in satire against friars (see Jill
Mann, *Chaucer and Medieval Estates Satire*, pp. 40–1) nor even a
greedy hypocrite like the friar in *The Summoner's Tale*. On a strictly
religious reading both he and the Monk corrupt the ideals of
their calling. Which do you think has the more serious faults, and

why? Is Chaucer's judgement influenced by considerations of personal attractiveness? The Appendix (page 183) contains a discussion of friars from William Langland's *Piers Plowman*. You may find it interesting to compare it with Chaucer's.

208 **wantowne** jolly, pleasure-loving (sometimes with a sexual implication).

209 A limiter (*lymytour*) is a friar licensed by his order to beg within a particular area.
solempne dignified.

210 There were four orders of friars: Dominicans, Franciscans, Carmelites and Augustinians.
kan knows.

211 **daliaunce** sociable talk (sometimes 'flirting').

212–13 Paying dowries to enable poor women to marry was regarded as a religious act of charity, but here the implication may be that the Friar is compensating women he has seduced.

214 What is the implication of this remark (and of the rhyme)?

216 **frankeleyns** landowners. (See line 331.)

219 **curat** parish priest. Sometimes friars were given special duties connected with confession, but *As seyde hymself* may imply that the Friar is making false claims to attract clients.

220 Whereas all parish priests could hear confession only those friars who were licensed (*licenciat*) by their order could do so.

221 On absolution and penance see Notes to the Pardoner (page 80). That the Friar heard confessions in a kindly manner (*swetely*) and was lenient (*esy* [223]) in giving penance may suit someone at the time of confession but may endanger the soul later (i.e. if the sinner is not fully contrite, or if he or she repeats the offence). Friars were often accused of becoming rich through the gratitude of those whose souls they had put at risk through their leniency, as if, in their hands, confession ceased to be a way of saving souls and became a way of making money.

224 **Ther** where.
pitaunce donation.

226 **wel yshryve** well confessed, truly sorry.

227 If a man gave, he (the Friar) dared to assert...

230 **hym soore smerte** he suffers painfully. Is his acceptance of payment kindly and realistic, or hypocritical and self-serving?

232 Friars were meant to be poor (*povre*) but in practice they often were not. Chaucer's Friar needed a substantial income to pay for marriages (212), presents (233–4), tavern bills (240) and fine clothes (261–2). (See Interpretations, page 115.)

233 **typet** dangling point of the hood.
farsed stuffed.

235–7 What do you make of the Friar's skill at secular music?

236 **rote** stringed instrument.

237 **yeddynges** songs. (Compare with line 266.)
baar outrely the pris absolutely took the prize.

238 **flour-de-lys** lily.

239 A champion represented someone else in a trial by combat.

241 **hostiler** innkeeper.
tappestere barmaid.

242 **lazar** leper.
beggestere beggar woman.

244 **facultee** professional dignity. What are we to make of Chaucer applying the words *worthy* (243) and *honest* (246) (honourable) to the Friar's refusal to associate with the poor and the sick?

246–7 **it may... poraille** there is no profit in dealing with such poor people.

248 **But al** but only.
vitaille victuals, food.

249 **over al** above all.
ther as where.

250 **lowely of servyse** humble in bearing. Compare his conduct among the wealthy to his attitude to the poor and the sick.

251 How are we to take *vertuous* here?

252 a–b The Friar paid a fee (*ferme*) for the right (*graunt*) to beg in his usual district (*haunt*). These lines appear in only a few manuscripts. It has been suggested that Chaucer withdrew them because they are inaccurate. No English limiter is known to have paid a fee in return for exclusive rights in his territory.

253 **sho** shoe (i.e. she was extremely poor).

254 **'In principio'** Latin for 'In the beginning' (the first words of the Gospel according to John).

255 **ferthyng**   see line 134.

256 A proverbial phrase implying excess profits. In this case probably his personal income (*purchas*) exceeded what he passed on to his friary (*rente*), but it could mean (following on from 252a) that the income he made from his district exceeded what he paid for exclusive rights.

257 **rage**   sport, frolic (sometimes with a sexual implication).
whelp   puppy.

258 **love-dayes**   days on which disputes were resolved.

259 **cloysterer**   monk.

260 A *cope* was a long cloak, the outer garment worn by monks and friars, sometimes seen as the distinctive mark of learned or Church men. Compare the Friar's clothes with those of the Monk and the Clerk.

261 **maister**   master of arts.

262 **double worstede**   thick, expensive cloth.
semycope   short cope. See note to line 260.

263 Round, like a bell fresh from its mould.

264 **lipsed**   lisped.
wantownesse   affectation.

267-8 What is the effect of this sudden and vivid comparison?

269 **cleped**   called.

The Merchant: Lines 270–284

Chaucer turns from the higher ranking ecclesiastical pilgrims to a group of secular figures associated with business, learning and the professions. The Merchant seems to be a large-scale businessman, involved in export (probably of cloth) and in the currency deals needed to finance exports. Chaucer only hints at the nature of the deals, which may suggest a reticence on the part of the Merchant. He describes the Merchant's appearance, conversation, and manner, hinting that he is much less prosperous than he seems. In this he differs from contemporary Estates Satire which tends to accuse merchants of avarice and excessive wealth. It is an understated portrait, suggesting a pompous man, with something to hide.

Chaucer may have known a lot about merchants, from his family background and from his work in the Custom House, but apart from the rather elusive reference to *sheeldes* (278) he avoids the display of technical knowledge which appears in his portraits of the Sergeant of the Law and the Doctor of Physic. There is evidence, particularly in Langland's poem, *Piers Plowman*, that contemporaries were troubled by the emergence of large-scale merchants.

270 **forked berd**   a beard divided into two parts. Portraits show that Chaucer himself followed this fashion. Is he making a joke by giving a devious character his own shape of beard?

271–3 **mottelee**   cloth of mixed colour, like a tweed. The Merchant's clothes, his expensive beaver-fur hat from Flanders and his boots elegantly (*fetisly*) clasped suggest wealth or the need to make a good first impression. (See Interpretations, pages 111–112).

274 **solempnely**   gravely, perhaps pompously.

275 **Sownynge**   associated with sound, especially musical sound. So it could mean that the Merchant is always talking about the money he makes or that the reasons he gives are always 'in accord with' the increase of his own profits.

276–7 He wanted the trading route between the ports of Middleburg, in the Netherlands, and Orwell, in Suffolk, kept open at all costs. Middleburg was the continental base of both associations of English merchants from 1384. Why should this be the main topic of the Merchant's political conversation?

278 **sheeld(es)**   the English translation of écu, either a unit of French currency or (more likely in this context) a Flemish 'money of account'. It used to be thought that the Merchant's currency dealings were illegal. The modern view is more complicated. The Merchant is selling in London bonds which he or his agents will have to redeem at a higher rate in Bruges. He obtains pounds to pay his present debts in England. By selling these bonds he is in effect borrowing money which he will have to repay in Bruges when he has sold his next shipment. This would be a legal way of managing a shortage

of cash but in the medieval view it is morally dubious (in that it is equivalent to paying interest). It also looks like a rather desperate move, mortgaging future profits in order to settle current debts.

279 **bisette** used.
281 **estatly** dignified.
 governaunce behaviour.
282 **bargaynes** deals (sales and purchases).
 chevyssaunce borrowing. (See Interpretations, pages 111–112.)
283–4 What are we to make of Chaucer's repetition of *worthy*, and of his saying that he does not know (*noot = ne woot*) his name?

The Clerk: Lines 285–308

The Clerk is a poor scholar, who is pursuing his studies at Oxford University. Since he has been studying for a long time, and since Chaucer mentions that he has not yet obtained a Church job (*benefice* [291]) presumably he is a priest. Why does Chaucer place him after the Merchant rather than before? Or why is he not beside the virtuous Parson? Perhaps Chaucer wanted to contrast his threadbare poverty with the wealth and pretension of the pilgrims on either side. Or perhaps placing him among the secular pilgrims fits in with the direction of his studies.

Chaucer's portrait concentrates on his poverty and his devotion to learning. His speech is brief, formal and moral. This contrasts with the students we meet in medieval satire and elsewhere in *The Canterbury Tales* (for example in *The Miller's Tale* and *The Reeve's Tale*), who are often boisterous, witty and lecherous. He is far less worldly than the other pilgrims, spending whatever money he has on books, which were very expensive in the fourteenth century. Do you think there may be some criticism of him as a 'perpetual student'? Or might we expect him to show more interest in Christian literature or in the religious duties he will take up when he finishes studying? At one point he suggests that his tale should be read as a religious allegory, but there are equally powerful indications that it is a human story about marriage.

286 'Who had been studying logic a long time before.' By the fourteenth century logic was the most important subject in the Bachelor of Arts degree, the first degree taken by all students. The skills taught in logic were used in the disputations and lectures which were required of those who wished to obtain higher degrees. Bachelors and Masters of Arts were also required to teach logic to undergraduates. Hence the Clerk still uses or teaches logic, even though he has moved on to higher studies.

289 **therto** also.
sobrely serious.

290 **overeste** uppermost.
courtepy jacket.

292 **office** secular job. Some priests took administrative posts in the service of great landowners.

293 **hym was levere** he would rather.

295 The works of the Greek philosopher Aristotle (384–322 BC) formed the basis of the arts course at medieval universities. The Clerk would have studied his books on logic, physics, biology, metaphysics, psychology and ethics. Twenty books (294) was a large private library. Books did not become really plentiful until printing (invented in the West *c*.1450) took over from manuscript copying towards the end of the fifteenth century.

296 **fithele** fiddle.
gay sautrie elegant psaltery (a stringed instrument, like a small harp).

297–8 Chaucer puns on two medieval meanings of 'philosopher': the advanced student of arts who has not yet moved on to theology, medicine or law (the three higher faculties in the medieval university system) and the alchemist, one who seeks the 'philosopher's stone' which will transmute base metal into gold.

299 **hente** obtain. Does Chaucer criticize the Clerk for spending

57

other people's money on books, or does his willingness to teach others save him from the charge of selfishness?

301 **bisily** earnestly.
    gan... preye prayed.
302 **scoleye** attend university.
304 **o** one.
305 **in forme and reverence** with formality and respect.
306 **quyk** vivid.
    hy sentence serious meaning.
307 **Sownynge** agreeing with, tending to. (See line 275.)

The Sergeant of the Law: Lines 309–330

Sergeants were a special group of very well-educated lawyers who had the exclusive right to plead in the Court of Common Pleas (one of the two highest courts in the land, the other being the King's Bench) and from whose ranks the judges were chosen. Usually they came from wealthy families. Chaucer emphasizes the Sergeant's knowledge of the law, his dignified appearance and his wealth.

What is the effect of Chaucer's use of the world *semed* (313, 322) meaning 'seemed'? Some critics see the portrait as strongly satirical, but Jill Mann (*Chaucer and Medieval Estates Satire*) points out that Chaucer avoids the complaints about the lawyer's greed and dishonesty found in estates satire. What conclusions do you draw from the portrait's emphasis on learning, honour and wealth, or from its lack of reference to justice?

310 **Parvys** probably the porch of St Paul's Cathedral, where clients consulted sergeants (or perhaps the porch of Westminster Hall, the seat of the courts).
311 **excellence** exceptional talent.
312 **Discreet** judicious.
    reverence dignity.
315 **patente** letter of appointment from the king.

pleyn commissioun full jurisdiction.

316 **science** knowledge.

   heigh renoun great reputation.

317 **fees and robes** annual payments from wealthy men to
   secure access to his services. What effect does Chaucer
   achieve by including so much legal terminology in the
   portrait?

318 **purchasour** land buyer. Does *greet* mean that he bought a
   lot, or that he was very good at it?

319 **fee symple** absolute possession; the clearest and most
   profitable form of land ownership.

320 **infect** be invalidated. The Sergeant was good at converting
   difficult leases and other complicated ownership arrangements
   into the advantageous condition of *fee symple* (319).

322 Why might he want to seem busier than he was?

323 **termes** law reports.

   caas cases.

   doomes judgements.

325 **endite** draw up.

326 **pynche at** find an error in. It has been suggested that this
   word refers to Thomas Pinchbeck, a sergeant whom Chaucer
   may well have known.

327 And he knew every statute completely by heart.

329 **Girt** encircled.

   ceint belt.

   barres stripes.

The Franklin: Lines 331–360

Helen Cooper in her Oxford Guide reports that the Franklin
causes the fiercest debate over any of the pilgrims. He 'can be
made to seem either the backbone of the social fabric or a man
in the grip of deadly sin, a glutton, proud and uncharitable'
(p.45). See the illustration of the Franklin from the Ellesmere
manuscript on page 123.

   A franklin was a 'free' (*franc*) man, a landowner without the
military obligations of the Knight, who ranked above him.

Chaucer's Franklin owns a good deal of land (339) and has held important judicial, political and administrative posts (355–9). The portrait links his careful pursuit of these duties with another characteristic of the English gentry: lavish feasting. Important men were expected to provide abundant hospitality and this was one way in which wealthy men from classes below the aristocracy could outshine their social superiors. How much is the Franklin's interest in food attractive? How much is it sinful? What are we to make of the ill-temper which this apparently gracious man can show towards his cook (351)?

331 Why do the Franklin and the Sergeant ride together? Is it because they have interests in common, or might they be striking some deal which will benefit them both?

332 How does the simile influence our view of the Franklin?

333 **complexioun** temperament. According to the medieval view the body contained four fluids or humours (blood, phlegm, yellow bile and black bile). The excess of one of these humours could lead to disease; the relative preponderance of one could dictate traits of character. Four types of character were recognized (sanguine, phlegmatic, choleric and melancholic) of which the sanguine (*sangwyn*) was considered the most happy. Although medicine has abandoned the theory of the four humours we still use these adjectives to describe character. (See also lines 420 and 587.)

334 A piece of bread (*sop*) in wine was a common breakfast.

335 **delit** delight, pleasure.
    wone custom.

336 Epicurus (341–270 BC) was a Greek philosopher who thought that pleasure was the highest purpose of life. For him the moral pleasures (such as friendship, or doing good to others) outweighed other kinds, but in the Middle Ages he was misrepresented as advocating unrestrained enjoyment of personal physical pleasure.

337–8 **pleyn delit... parfit** pure pleasure was true perfect happiness.

340 Julian the Hospitaller was the (legendary) patron saint of innkeepers.

341 **after oon**   of uniformly good quality.

342 **envyned**   stocked with wine.

345 How does this metaphor affect our view of the Franklin?

347 **After**   according to.
   sondry   various. Seasonal change of diet was considered to
   be a good way of keeping the humours (333) in balance and
   thus of remaining healthy.

349 **muwe**   pen for birds.

350 **breem**   freshwater bream.
   luce   pike.
   stuwe   fish pond.

352 **Poynaunt**   sharp, spicy.
   geere   cutlery.

353 His table was left permanently in place (*dormant*) in the hall,
   the main public room of his house. Since tables were usually
   taken down after meals (so that the hall could be used for
   other purposes) this observation confirms that food was the
   Franklin's top priority.

355–6 He presided at law courts (*sessiouns*), presumably as a Justice of
   the Peace, and represented his county in Parliament. Chaucer
   himself undertook both these responsibilities on occasion.

357 **anlaas**   dagger.
   gipser   purse.

359 He had served his county both as sheriff, chief officer of the
   crown, and as *contour*, overseer of the collection of taxes.

360 **vavasour**   (sub-vassal) is a technical term for the lowest rank
   of the nobility. Chaucer may mean that the Franklin
   surpassed the local nobility or that he had crossed the barrier
   into the higher class. In the late fourteenth century people
   could be awarded noble (*gentil*) status in return for service to
   the crown, as happened to Chaucer's own family.

The Five Guildsmen: Lines 361–378

The Five Guildsmen represent the growing economic importance
of shopkeepers and small manufacturers. The poll tax of 1379
assessed aldermen at the same rate as barons, merchants with

knights. The wealth of Chaucer's Guildsmen entitles them to a leading position in the religious confraternity (364) whose ceremonial livery they wear. Why does Chaucer treat all five of them together? Do you think he satirizes their pride, or pays tribute to their prominent role in society? What does he think of their wives (374–8)?

361 **Haberdasshere** haberdasher; seller of hats, caps and small items connected with dress, such as thread and tape.

362 **Webbe** weaver.
Tapycer weaver of tapestries and rugs.

364 **fraternitee** religious organization for lay people. Confraternities (or guilds) maintained chapels, and arranged burials, masses for the dead, and material social benefits. They also performed charitable works, for the benefit of their members' souls, including paying for schools. Some guilds united those who practised one particular trade, which the guild would control (e.g. by establishing standards of workmanship and regulating apprenticeships and admission to the trade). Such guilds were the forerunners of modern employers' organizations and trades unions.

365 **geere** equipment.
apiked trimmed.

366 **chaped** mounted. The silver ornaments on their knives, belts and purses indicate a display of wealth and status. Such ornaments were forbidden to merchants and citizens unless they possessed property to the value of £500.

367 **clene** brightly, splendidly.

369 **burgeys** burgess, member of the city council. The guildhall (*yeldehalle* [370]) is the seat of the city government whose officials would sit on the dais (*deys* [370]).

371–2 Does Chaucer say that the Guildsmen possess (*kan*) the wisdom fitting (*shaply*) for aldermen, the highest ranking city officials, or do we hear the voices of the Guildsmen's own ambitions? Is Chaucer looking down on them from his higher social position?

373 **catel** goods, property.
rente income.

375 Is Chaucer confirming the Guildsmen's right to become
aldermen, or do we hear the voices of their wives urging them
on? Or is the phrase ironic?

376 Aldermen's wives were entitled to be called (*ycleped*) 'madam'.

377 **vigilies**   vigils, religious services and feasts held on the eve of
a saint's day.
bifore   in front (of the procession). (Compare with line 450.)

378 **mantel**   cloak.
roialliche ybore   carried, like royalty.

The Cook: Lines 379–387

Estates satire did not provide Chaucer with any models to draw
on in portraying the Cook. The list of dishes and techniques
seems to indicate his appreciation of the Cook's skill. But what
does he think of his ulcer, probably (in the medieval view) the
result of intemperate or unhygienic habits? Why does he
mention the Cook's knowledge of London ale? In the prologue
to his unfinished tale we learn that the Cook's name is Roger,
that he originally came from Ware in Hertfordshire, and that he
now has a shop in London. The Host accuses him of selling pies
which have been reheated twice.

379 **for the nones**   for the occasion. This Cook is not regularly
employed by any of the Guildsmen. He is an independent
businessman who has hired himself out to them for the
duration of the pilgrimage. What does their hiring of the
Cook tell us about the Guildsmen's attitude to their
pilgrimage?

381 **poudre-marchant tart**   a sharp-flavoured spice.
galyngale   a root used in flavouring.

383 **sethe**   simmer.

384 **mortreux**   thick soup or stew.

385 **harm**   pity.
as it thoughte me   as it seemed to me.

386 **shyne**   shin.
mormal   ulcer, running sore. (See Interpretations, page 91.)

What is the effect of prefacing this observation with an
expression of pity? Or of placing these lines at this point in
the portrait?

387 **blankmanger**   a mousse made of chopped chicken (or fish)
with rice.

The Shipman: Lines 388–410

The Shipman is a thief (396–7) and a murderer (400). His face is
weatherbeaten (394) and he lacks the grace of a good horseman
(390). But he is brave, experienced and skilful at navigation
(401–5). He knows all the harbours of north-west Europe (407).
Does Chaucer condemn the good captain for being a bad man? Is
his vice unavoidable? Or is his skill so rare and necessary as to
outweigh his crimes? Because Chaucer specifies that the Shipman
sails the *Magdalen* (*Maudelayne* [410]) out of Dartmouth,
scholars have tried to identify an original for this portrait (the
current candidates are Piers Risselden and John Piers) but there
is no general agreement.

390 **rouncy**   cart-horse.
   as he kouthe   as best he could.
391 **faldyng**   coarse woollen cloth.
395 **felawe**   companion. Notice how Chaucer attaches this to
   what looks like drinking and turns out to be theft.
397 **Burdeux-ward**   from the direction of Bordeaux.
   chapman   merchant (here the agent who accompanies the
   shipment).
398 **nyce**   scrupulous.
   keep   notice.
400 He drowned the crew of the other vessel. This was a common
   way of disposing of the witnesses to piracy. What does this
   euphemism tell us about the Shipman? Would we expect
   Chaucer to condemn the Shipman's behaviour more strongly?
401–3 The Shipman is skilful at reckoning tides, currents and
   other hazards. He knows his harbours, the influence of the
   moon on tides, and how to pilot a ship (*lodemenage*). What

is the relationship between this sentence and the previous one?

404 **Cartage** perhaps Cartagena in Spain, rather than Carthage in North Africa, since it was nearer to the routes which English captains sailed at this time.

405 **wys to undertake** prudent in his undertakings.

408 **Gootlond** probably Gotland, an island off the Swedish coast, though it might be Jutland, part of modern Denmark. Probably *Fynystere* is Cape Finisterre in northern Spain rather than Finistère in Brittany.

409 **cryke** creek, inlet.
Britaigne Brittany.

410 **barge** a sea-going merchant vessel.

The Doctor of Physic: Lines 411–444

We are told that the Doctor of Physic has read the works of a large number of medical authorities (429–34) and that he understands all the methods of diagnosis and treatment favoured by his contemporaries (419–24). He is also well-dressed and miserly (439–41). Chaucer suggests that he receives commission from apothecaries (427) and hints at his atheism (438). But medieval satire usually treated doctors far more harshly than this, accusing them of deceitful incompetence, greed and lack of care for their patients. Do you see the portrait as critical or neutral? Can you think of anything positive in it? One would expect the Doctor to be placed beside the Sergeant or the Merchant. By associating him with the Shipman might Chaucer be making implications about the Doctor's morals or about his effect on his patients?

411–13 Chaucer's Doctor of Physic has the rare accomplishment of a doctorate in medicine. This necessitated many years of study on the continent. Surgery was often considered to be a separate and inferior skill, partly within the province of the barber.

413 **To speke of** in respect of, or perhaps 'for speaking of'.

414 Medical science was grounded in astronomy in the sense that the position of the stars when someone was born (their horoscope) would determine the balance of humours (see 333) within them. Equally, by considering the position of the planets at the moment when a disease began the physician would work out which humour was in excess and when it would be most propitious to intervene (by, for example, bloodletting or applying leeches) to draw off the humour which was in excess. In the Middle Ages the science of astronomy included what we now call astrology (and regard as superstition).

416 **houres** may mean hours or stages of the disease, or astrological hours in which different planets had predominance.
magyk natureel beneficent magic, involving co-operation with nature, as opposed to black magic, which involved calling up demons.

417 **fortunen the ascendent** either calculate the position of the planets or position the planet coming over the horizon (*ascendent*) favourably for the patient. This refers to the practice of making talismans (*ymages* [418]) at auspicious moments. The talismans (and, in theory, the influence they preserved) would be applied to a part of the patient's body which was in need of help.

420 This line refers to the four humours (see lines 333 and 414): blood (hot and moist), phlegm (cold and moist), yellow bile (hot and dry) and black bile (cold and dry).

421 The excess of a particular humour originated (*engendred*) in a specific part of the body. Medieval physicians used elaborate tables which assigned parts of the body to particular humours and particular planets.

422 **praktisour** practitioner. Is Chaucer's judgement here the same as in his parallel remark about the Knight (72)?

423 Once he knew the cause of the disease and the source of its ill effects.

424 **Anon** at once.
boote remedy, medication.

425 **apothecaries** pharmacists.

426 **letuaries** electuaries, medicines.

427 **wynne** profit. What is the effect of linking the mention of remedies to the profitable collaboration of doctor and pharmacist?

429–34 Chaucer provides an extremely long list of medical authorities, among them: Aesculapius (*Esculapius*), the god who founded medicine according to Greek legend; Dioscorides Paedianus (*Deyscorides*), flourished in the first century AD, whose *Materia Medica* attempts to provide a systematic description of the medicines available to a doctor; Hippocrates (*Ypocras*), flourished in the fifth century BC, who used to be considered the author of the early Greek medical writings, the so-called *Hippocratic Corpus*; Rufus of Ephesus (*Rufus*); Galen (*Galyen*), 129–199 AD, Greek philosopher and author of the most influential ancient medical works; the Islamic medical authorities Ali ibn Abbas (*Haly*), died 994, and Rhazes (*Razis*), c. 854–930; the Islamic Aristotelian philosophers Avicenna (*Avycen*), 980–1037, and Averroes (*Averrois*), 1126–1198; Constantine the African (*Constantyn*), flourished 1065–1085, who translated medical works from Arabic; and some medieval English medical authorities, Bernard of Gordon (*Bernard*), flourished 1283–1309, John of Gaddesden (*Gatesden*), died around 1349, and Gilbertus Anglicus (*Gilbertyn*), flourished 1250. (The identity of *Serapion* is in dispute; Johannes Damascenus [*Damascien*] is given as the author of some medical books now known to have been written by others.) Why are there so many names? Is Chaucer poking fun at intellectual pedantry, or is he assuring us that this man really is a fine physician?

435 **mesurable** moderate.

436 **superfluitee** excess. Medieval authorities stress the influence of diet on health. Is the Doctor of Physic practising what he preaches, or does he put his own health before his patients'?

438 What are the implications of the Doctor's limited Bible reading?

439 **sangwyn** red (with a pun on the humour).
pers grey-blue.

440 Taffeta and sendal were types of silk, which was expensive.

441 **but esy of dispence** only moderate in spending.

442 **wan** won, earned.

> **pestilence**   time of plague.
443 **cordial**   medicine for the heart. Why does the Doctor of
Physic especially like gold? (See Interpretations, pages
112–113.)

The Wife of Bath: Lines 445–476

Strictly *wif* means woman (as opposed to maiden) rather than
wife, but Alison is so famous as the *Wife* of Bath that it would be
pedantry to call her anything else. Chaucer's portrait
concentrates on the Wife's sexuality, her trade, her extravagant
clothing, her pride, her love of pilgrimages, and the effects of age
on her. But these subjects are so intertwined that each reflects on
the others and a composite impression animates all the separate
details. Chaucer begins with her deafness (to elicit pity) but
quickly moves on to ask us to admire the excellence of her
weaving, and also to take pride in it since it surpasses the work
of the weavers of Ypres and Ghent. In parallel to this, though we
admire it less, there is her pride in her status within her own
parish (and her determination to maintain it against the
aspirations of other women). Her anger is commented on (and
also softened) by the description of her absurd Sunday hats
which weigh ten pounds. What is the effect of the rhyme which
links the *worthy womman* (459) to the five husbands? What is the
effect of Chaucer's use of the word *worthy* here? (Compare the
way he uses it of the Knight [43] or the Merchant [279].) How
does the audience react to the *oother compaignye* (461) who are not
to be mentioned for now? Admiration, amusement, sympathy,
outrage, broad laughter and mild censure succeed each other in
this portrait. Satire against women contributes details to the
portrait but the bitter effect of satire is absent from it. Anyone
who wants to know more about the Wife's life and opinions will
enjoy the long prologue to her tale. The portrait given here is
consistent with that but different and independently delightful.
(See Interpretations, pages 133–138).

A medieval moralist might denounce her sins. Which of the seven deadly sins (pride, envy, lechery, anger, gluttony, avarice and sloth) do you think she is guilty of? Do you think Chaucer condemns her? Why does he mention her large hips, her laughter, her wide-set teeth, her deafness and details of her clothing? See the illustration of the Wife from the Ellesmere manuscript on page 136.

446 **somdel deef** somewhat deaf.
     scathe pity.
447 **haunt** skill.
448 Flemish weavers, and especially those from Ypres and Ghent, were usually considered to be superior to British ones.
450 Worshippers used to go to the altar individually to present their offerings. Arguments about precedence were quite common.
452 When she is *out of alle charitee*, does charity denote the gift which she was about to present for the poor, the way she ought to treat her neighbours, or her love for God?
453 **coverchiefs** headcoverings.
     ground texture.
457 **streite yteyd** tightly laced.
     moyste supple.
461 **Withouten** not counting.
463–6 She has been to the most famous and most distant pilgrimage sites. At Jerusalem she would have seen the places associated with the death and resurrection of Christ, at Rome the chief basilicas of the city which commemorate the martyrdom of the leaders of the early Christian Church (including St Peter and St Paul), at Boulogne an image of the Virgin Mary, at Santiago de Compostela in Galicia (north-west Spain) the shrine of St James, and at Cologne the shrines of the three wise men and of St Ursula and the 11,000 virgins said to have been martyred with her. Is Chaucer here poking fun at the Wife's excesses or emphasizing her extreme devotion, in making such long and expensive journeys? Or did she have other motives for going on pilgrimages? (See Interpretations, pages 96, 99.)

464 **straunge strem**   foreign river.

467 Does *wandrynge by the weye* refer to her experience of travel,
or is there a (more critical) moral implication?

468 **Gat-tothed**   her teeth were widely spaced. In her own
prologue the Wife says that this facial feature fits in with her
strong sexual desires. What is the effect of linking this line by
rhyme to the *wandrynge* in the line above?

469 **amblere**   ambling horse.
easily   comfortably.

470 A wimple covers the head and neck, leaving the face visible.

472 **foot-mantel**   overskirt.

475 **love**   i.e. lovesickness.
per chaunce   as it happened.

476 **koude**   knew.
olde daunce   tricks of the trade.

The Parson: Lines 477–528

Chaucer emphasizes the Parson's strict fulfilment of the
instructions of the gospel (481, 498, 527), his kindness to his
parishioners (487, 518), and his devoted concern for them (492,
512). He must be an example as well as a guide (497). From
Chaucer's discussion of what his Parson avoids we also learn a
good deal about the vices prevalent among parish clergy (living
far from the parish [509], corruption [507, 514], excessive
concern with tithes [486]). Compare Chaucer's use of this
material to William Langland's criticism of corrupt parish clergy
in *Piers Plowman* (see Appendix, page 183). From time to time
we seem to hear the Parson's own voice, making an analogy
or drawing a lesson (499–506, 513, 519). Should the Parson's
virtues be used to judge the other pilgrims? Or does the
narrator's expression of approval for so many of the pilgrims (at
least in their own terms) make it impossible for us to apply the
Parson's standards to the others? Why does Chaucer place
the Parson just after the Wife of Bath? See the illustration from
the Ellesmere manuscript on page 115.

486 People were supposed to pay a tenth (*tithe*) of their income to support the parish priest and the Church. The penalty for non-payment was excommunication, exclusion from the services of the Church and from the spiritual community of Christian souls. But Chaucer's Parson was very reluctant (*Ful looth*) to impose this penalty, which, if unrevoked, would result in the damnation (hence *cursen*) of the person involved.

489 From what the people gave him and from his Church income.

490 He knew how to be content with little.

492 **lefte nat** did not omit.
      for in spite of.

494 **muche and lite** great and small.

499 **figure** figure of speech. The figures of speech were listed in the art of rhetoric, which was widely taught in medieval schools and universities. In the Middle Ages there was a special type of rhetoric textbook which taught the art of composing sermons.

502 **lewed man** uneducated man.

506 **clennesse** purity.

507–14 As a result of the Black Death (1349) the population of many parishes was reduced and the price of grain fell. This severely reduced the incomes of parish priests. Many responded by leaving their parishes to work for guilds (see 364) or landowners, singing masses for the souls of the dead or working as administrators.

507 **benefice** Church job. Some priests would keep the income from a parish but hire someone else at a lower rate to perform the duties required.

509 In St Paul's Cathedral there were many chantries: jobs of singing masses for the souls of the dead. A rich person or a guild might provide money for this purpose since prayers and masses said on someone's behalf would help the soul pass through purgatory and on into heaven more rapidly.

511 To be employed by a confraternity (see 364).

514 **mercenarie** hireling. The Parson works out of a sense of responsibility and not merely for money. Commentators compare John 10:12, 'He that is an hireling, and not the shepherd, whose own the sheep are not, seeth the wolf coming, and leaveth the sheep and fleeth'. In the Latin Bible,

the Vulgate, the equivalent for 'hireling' in this passage is *mercenarius*.

516 **despitous** scornful.

517 **daungerous** and **digne** both mean haughty, aloof.

519 **fairnesse** gentle means.

520 **bisynesse** endeavour.

521 **But** unless, except.

523 **snybben** rebuke.
nonys occasion, time.

525 **waited after** expected.
reverence ceremony

526 **spiced** over-particular. The priest did not give undue importance to minor sins, or did not worry about the technical details, but concentrated on essential Christian teaching.

The Ploughman: Lines 529–544

The Ploughman combines agricultural labour (the occupation of the vast majority of the population) with sincere religious devotion. He works hard out of duty as much as for his own advantage (531, 537). He follows Christ's two commandments (Mark 12:30–1), loving God first, and then loving his neighbour as much as himself (533–5). The relationship between Parson and Ploughman reflects the ideal of a cohesive and religious society, in which people's conduct was based on a sense of unchanging obligations. (See Interpretations, pages 114–115, 119.) Commentators have pointed out that the relationship between the Ploughman and the Parson is very different from the relationships between other pilgrims. They have suggested that other alliances in the *General Prologue* are more short-term, entered into for mutual benefit, and dissoluble when those benefits disappear. Paul Strohm, in *Social Chaucer*, argues that this aspect of the *General Prologue* reflects a change in English society, from a structured and religious state based on eternal obligations towards a society based on short-term dissoluble contracts.

530 **ylad**   hauled.
   dong   manure.
   fother   cartload.
534 At all times, whether in pleasure or in pain.
536 **dyke**   make ditches.
   delve   dig.
539 That the ploughman paid tithes (486) indicates that he was a
   free man with a plot of land of his own. Most agricultural
   labourers were serfs. Critics have pointed out that the
   pilgrimage includes no representative of the highest ranks of
   society and no one from the lowest (the vast majority) either.
540 **propre swynk**   own labour.
   catel   property, possessions.
541 **mere**   mare.
544 Is it significant that Chaucer names himself among five
   rogues? Or might it be a conventional gesture of politeness,
   placing himself last?

The Miller: Lines 545–566

In contrast to the moral emphasis of the two preceding portraits,
the Miller is described overwhelmingly in physical terms. He is
strong and ugly, loud and foul-mouthed, and he cheats his
customers. Can you find anything redeeming in this portrait?
How would you compare the Miller with the Doctor of Physic
or the Shipman? And yet the Miller tells one of the most
delightful of all the tales, combining realistic description and a
low view of human motivation with subtle and imaginative
comedy. Perhaps Chaucer liked the bagpipes.

545 **stout carl**   strong rogue; (*carl* has undertones of vice, like
   other words for the lower classes, such as churl or villain).
   for the nones   indeed.
547 **over al ther he cam**   wherever he went.
548 The ram would be the prize in the wrestling competition.
549 It is hard to reconcile *short-sholdred* with *brood* and *thikke*.

Perhaps his forearms or his neck were short while his shoulders were broad. *Knarre* usually means 'crag', so perhaps 'rugged man'.

550 **nolde heve of harre** would not lift off its hinges.

552 What is the effect of comparing (parts of) the Miller to a sow (twice), a fox, a spade and an oven?

552–7 The medieval science of physiognomy aimed to determine people's character and morality on the basis of their faces. You can imagine how useful it would be to know what people are like just from looking at them! In the medieval manuals, red hair and large nostrils (*nosethirles* [557]) were said to indicate anger, foolishness and lechery. A large mouth suggested gluttony and boldness. W.C. Curry has described the physiognomical implications of the Miller's face in detail in his *Chaucer and the Medieval Sciences*.

555 **werte** wart.

toft of herys tuft of hairs.

558 **bokeler** small shield.

bar carried, wore.

559 **forneys** oven, or perhaps cauldron.

560 **janglere** chatterer, teller of tales.

goliardeys buffoon, joker.

561 **harlotries** indecency.

562 **tollen thries** take three times the accepted payment. Farmers paid millers a proportion of the flour milled.

563 Millers judged grain with their thumbs, so a golden thumb might connect his profits with his skill. But there is also an allusion to the proverb: *an honest miller hath a golden thumb*, which implies that there were no honest millers. (See Interpretations, page 145.)

565 **sowne** play, sound.

The Manciple: Lines 567–586

A manciple's job was to purchase supplies of food for an institution, such as a college, a monastery or, as here, one of the Inns of Court (*temple* [567]). The Inns of Court are organizations of barristers which also act as law schools. Chaucer tells us that the Manciple is crafty enough to cheat his employers, who are themselves clever enough to run any estate in England. He does not say what he does with the money he embezzles. In general we learn remarkably little about the Manciple, which may itself be significant.

567 Is Chaucer being ironic when he describes the Manciple as *gentil* (noble)?

570 **by taille** on credit, from the tally-stick, on which such transactions were recorded. The stick was split so that both creditor and debtor had an identical record.

571 **Algate** always.
wayted watched, took care.
achaat buying.

572 **ay biforn** always ahead (i.e. in profit).

573 In what way would it be God's grace that an uneducated person could trick many learned people?

574 **lewed** uneducated.
pace surpass.

577 **curious** skilful.

581 **propre good** own wealth.

582 **but if** unless.
wood mad.

583 Or live as economically as he wished.

586 **sette hir aller cappe** deceived them all. How does Chaucer's long account of the abilities of his victims affect our attitude to the Manciple's deceptions?

The Reeve: Lines 587–622

Normally a reeve was responsible for the practical part of estate management, checking on the condition of the lord's land and animals, and supervising the labour of his tenants. Chaucer's Reeve has also acquired some of the duties of the bailiff, supervising the stores (593), calculating the likely yield of the harvest (595), and presenting the accounts (600). We are told that he performs these duties well. Is he also corrupt, or does he merely oppress his fellow servants? Why are they so frightened of him (605)? How has he become able to lend money to his master (611)? The Reeve's thinness and his craftiness fit in with the humour (see Notes, page 60, line 333) of a choleric (*colerik*) man (587) but he lacks the equally characteristic emotional instability. Do you find any evidence of the choleric person's bad temper? Compare Chaucer's treatment of the Reeve with his attitude to the Manciple.

590 **top**   top of his head.
    dokked   cut short. Why does Chaucer give so much emphasis to his short hair?
592 **Ylyk a staf**   like a staff.
593 **gerner**   granary.
    bynne   grain bin.
594 **on him wynne**   get the better of him.
596 **yeldynge**   yield.
597 **neet**   cattle.
    dayerye   dairy cattle.
598 **swyn**   pigs.
    stoor   livestock.
602 No one could prove that he owed anything.
603 **nas**   (= *ne was*) was not.
    baillif   farm manager, usually a reeve's superior but here responsible to him.
    hierde   herdsman.
    hyne   servant.
604 **sleighte**   tricks.
    covyne   deceit.
606 Why does the Reeve live away from other people?
609 **riche**   richly.
    astored   provided.
610 **subtilly**   cunningly. The Reeve lends the lord his own money (*good* [611]), which he has embezzled.
612 The coat and hood will be the Reeve's reward.
613 Why does Chaucer say that the Reeve once learned a good trade (*myster*)?

616 **pomely** dappled.
   highte was called. Scot was a common name for a horse (*stot* [615]), especially in Norfolk.
618 Why is his knife rusty?
620 Bawdeswell (*Baldeswelle*) is in Norfolk, about 15 miles north-west of Norwich. Some scholars have been encouraged to look for a real-life model for the Reeve by the fact that Chaucer was once slightly involved in a court case about the manor of Bawdeswell.
621 **Tukked** (his coat was) hitched up.
622 **route** company. Does he ride at the back to avoid his enemy the Miller or because the rear is the best place from which to observe the other pilgrims? Does it matter that Chaucer here (and elsewhere) describes the pilgrims' behaviour on the journey which they have not yet begun?

The Summoner: Lines 623–668

In fourteenth-century England, ecclesiastical courts existed alongside the civil courts. Ecclesiastical courts, which were often presided over by the archdeacon (655), tried churchmen for all offences except treason, and tried lay people for offences against the Church such as non-payment of tithes, heresy and adultery. The civil courts tried lay people for all other offences against person, property and the state. Summoners were lay officials employed by the Church courts to deliver summonses to attend court and sometimes to provide information about wrongdoers. Many lay people resented the Church courts, and summoners were often satirized. They were accused of lechery because of their involvement in cases of adultery.

Chaucer describes the Summoner's corrupt practices, and attacks his drunkenness and his ignorance. But the portrait is overshadowed by the Summoner's facial disfigurement. Does Chaucer's description make you feel sympathetic or disgusted? What do you think of his explanation for the disease? Are we meant to draw a parallel between the Summoner's appearance and his moral state? Unusually, Chaucer dissociates himself from this pilgrim's opinions (659). Why? What should we think of the Summoner's 'good fellowship' and the mercy he shows to some sinners? What is the effect of his garland and his bread shield (666–8)?

624 **cherubynnes** cherub's. Cherubim are angels of the second rank. Usually they are depicted as blue (seraphim are red) but some medieval authors confused the orders of angels. The angels' redness was thought to be caused by the flames of divine love. What causes the Summoner's red face? Is Chaucer being ironic when he compares him to an angel? Perhaps the (slight) similarity between the roles makes the comparison funnier?

625 **saucefleem** covered with pimples. In *Chaucer and the Medieval Sciences*, W.C. Curry argues that the pimples, the narrow (*narwe*) eyes and the loss of hair (627) indicate that the Summoner suffers from alopecia, a form of leprosy. Other scholars have made different diagnoses (scabies or syphilis).

626 From early Greek literature onwards the sparrow (*sparwe*) has been said to be lecherous.

627 **scalled** scabby (scall is a skin disease).
piled hairless.

629–30 Mercury (*quyk-silver*), lead monoxide (*lytarge*), sulphur (*brymstoon*), borax (*Boras*), white lead (*ceruce*) and cream of tartar (*oille of tartre*) are all possible treatments for skin diseases. Chaucer here uses technical language not, as he usually does, to show the pilgrim's knowledge but rather to emphasize the seriousness of the disease. (See Interpretations, page 121.)

631 **byte** burn, scour.

632 **whelkes** pimples.

634–5 Medieval people thought that garlic, leeks and red wine would heat the blood and thus worsen diseases like the Summoner's. (Compare with line 626.)

636 **wood** mad.

638 It was proverbial that some people spoke Latin when drunk.

Presumably most of them knew more phrases than the Summoner.

640 **decree**   decretal, a legally binding statement by a pope, hence a law of the Church.

642 Many medieval texts mention jays being taught to imitate human speech. Equally the continual noise of the jay is often called 'chatter'.

643 **clepen**   say.

'Watte'   a shortened form of Walter. Perhaps Chaucer thinks of *Watte* as the sound a jay makes. Or perhaps *pope* together with *jay* (642) alludes to 'popinjay' (sometimes 'papejay'), a parrot, which could be taught to imitate speech.

644 **grope**   test, question.

645 **philosophie**   learning.

646 **'Questio quid iuris'**   Latin for 'the question is which part of the law?' A lawyer might use this phrase in court, but the Summoner says it because it is an all-purpose remark.

647 **harlot**   rascal. In what sense does Chaucer call him *gentil* and *kynde*?

649 **suffre**   allow (i.e. he would ignore the offence).

for   in return for.

651 **atte fulle**   completely.

652 Some scholars explain this expression as 'trick someone', others as 'seduce a woman'.

654 **awe**   fear. The Summoner assures the sinner that if he pays up he need have no fear of being reported to the ecclesiastical court, or of the penalties there. There may be an implication (658) that even if the case comes to court the archdeacon can be bribed. (See Interpretations, pages 116–121.)

655 **curs**   excommunication (compare 486).

659 Might this be a line in which we hear Chaucer speaking as author rather than as pilgrim?

660–1 'Every guilty man should fear excommunication because that will damn (literally, kill) as surely as absolution will save.' (See Notes to the Pardoner, page 80.)

662 **war hym**   let him beware.

Significavit   writ of imprisonment (so called from the opening word of the document, which would be in Latin for the Church courts).

663 **In daunger**   in (his) control.
   at his owene gise   as he pleased.
664 **girles**   can refer to young people of both sexes.
665 **conseil**   secrets.
   al hir reed   advisor to all of them.
668 **cake**   loaf of bread. Does Chaucer mean to suggest that the
   Summoner is a glutton, or a fool, or is it a (possibly
   endearing) eccentricity to carry a loaf instead of a shield?

The Pardoner: Lines 669–714

Pardoners were employees of the Church, often priests, who
sold pardons (or indulgences). In the medieval view, every sinful
act had two aspects, an eternal aspect which involved turning
away from God, and a temporal aspect which involved
turning towards the world. If a sinner confessed his or her sins
fully and showed contrition, a priest would give absolution,
which is forgiveness for the eternal part of the sin, and a penance,
which would compensate for the temporal part. A penance
would usually be an act of charity or of devotion (such as saying
a set number of prayers or visiting a particular shrine). It was
possible to obtain, from the Pope or from a bishop, an
indulgence to remove some or all of one's temporal guilt. An
indulgence might be granted for exceptional help to the Church
or in return for money.

The sale of indulgences became a way of converting guilt
into income for the Church. The system was often abused and
was much criticized. Indeed the abuse of indulgences was one of
the factors which precipitated the Reformation of the sixteenth
century, when the Church was split. One of the actions of the
Council of Trent (1545–63), which reformed the Catholic
Church, was to end the sale of indulgences.

Chaucer follows William Langland in *Piers Plowman* (see
Appendix, pages 183–185) and other social satirists in making his
Pardoner exploit his occupation for personal financial gain.
Beyond that the Pardoner makes money by charging people for

seeing or touching false relics which he carries around (694–704). Chaucer implies that his man is such an excellent pardoner (693) *because* he tricks people so outrageously and makes so much money. On the other hand he praises the quality of the Pardoner's participation in church services. Compare Chaucer's attitude to his Pardoner with Langland's.

Much critical attention has been devoted to the Pardoner's appearance and his sexual inclination. W.C. Curry in *Chaucer and the Medieval Sciences* argued that the Pardoner was a eunuch and that he and the Summoner were homosexual partners. The main evidence in favour of this view is: the thinness and length of the Pardoner's hair (675–9), his high-pitched voice (688), his lack of a beard (689), Chaucer's belief that he was *a geldyng or a mare* (691), a possible pun involving their singing (673), the song sung (672) and the supposed medieval belief that the hare is a hermaphrodite (684). The interpretation of much of this evidence is disputed. The main alternative view is that the Pardoner was an effeminate heterosexual like the character Absolon in *The Miller's Tale*. In support of this one might cite the Pardoner's claim in his own prologue that he has a woman in every town. It has also been pointed out that the Pardoner must at most only have appeared to be a eunuch because a real eunuch could not be a priest (708–12). According to D.R. Howard in *Chaucer, His Life, His Works, His World* there is no evidence that the word *mare* (691) could mean 'male homosexual'. Some critics' attempts to connect the Pardoner's appearance with his sexual orientation probably involve stereotyping and an unconscious hostility to homosexuals.

669 Why does Chaucer call the Pardoner *gentil*?
670 The Hospital of St Mary of Rouncesval (Chaucer's *Rouncivale*) at Charing Cross, an Augustinian friary, was very active in the sale of indulgences and was involved in scandals over unauthorized sales in the 1380s. Chaucer's audience would probably have picked up the association of dishonesty.
compeer comrade.

671 Who had come directly from the papal court.

672 Probably a refrain from a popular song.

673 **stif burdoun** strong bass accompaniment (some critics find a phallic pun).

675 In physiognomy (see Notes to lines 552–7, page 74) yellow hair was said to indicate wild and unruly behaviour, thin hair guile and covetousness.

676 **strike** hank.
      flex flax.

677 **ounces** small strands.

679 **colpons** strands.

681 **trussed** packed.
      walet travel bag.

682 **Hym thoughte** it seemed to him.
      jet fashion.

683 **Dischevelee** with hair unbound.
      bare bare-headed.

684 **glarynge eyen** bulging eyes.

685 **vernycle** a badge from the pilgrimage to Rome. The badge depicts St Veronica's handkerchief (kept in St Peter's) which is believed to carry an imprint of Christ's face.

687 **Bretful** brimful. Is there an ironic or mercenary implication in saying that the pardons were hot from Rome?

688 **smal** high-pitched.

691 How do you interpret this line?

692 **craft** trade. Berwick-on-Tweed is on the border with Scotland. Ware is just north of London. So presumably Chaucer means 'across the whole country'. (But there might perhaps be an anti-northern joke. Chaucer's associations were with Kent.)

694 **male** bag.
      pilwe-beer pillowcase. Most medieval people venerated relics associated with Christ and the saints, but satirists often claimed that they were false, as most of them must have been.

695 **Oure Lady** the Virgin Mary, mother of Christ.

696 **gobet** piece.

698 **hente** took (in the sense of 'called him').

699 **latoun** latten, brass.

702 **person** parson.

    upon lond   in the country. Is Chaucer making a comment here by reminding us of his Parson and suggesting a comparison?

703 **gat hym**   obtained.

706 **apes**   fools, dupes.

707 **atte laste**   finally. What is the effect of *trewely*?

708 Does the Pardoner's reading, singing and preaching really make him a *noble ecclesiaste* in church? Might his high goat-like voice (688) suggest that there is some irony here?

710 The priest sings the offertory while the congregation give money. (Compare with 450–2.) Why does the Pardoner sing this part of the service best of all?

712 What does the phrase about smoothing (*affile*) his tongue to *wynne silver* (713) make us think of the Pardoner?

Explanation and apology: Lines 715–746

At the end of the portraits Chaucer reminds us that he has told us all about the pilgrims and why they have come to Southwark, and he sets out the rest of his plan. First, he will narrate what happened on the evening that the company met, and then he will describe the pilgrimage itself. But before beginning he makes an elaborate apology. It will not be his fault if the language, stories and behaviour of the pilgrims are not always polite. His duty is to describe what happened. It is possible to read this section (725–42) almost as a statement of Chaucer's poetic creed: absolute fidelity to what was said, or, given the fictional status of the whole pilgrimage, absolute appropriateness (hence *properly* [729]) to character (or narrative?). But the paragraph can also be read as an attempt to evade responsibility for what he has created: do not blame me for the bad taste and bad language which follows, I am only reporting what was said.

    Chaucer also wants to apologize for not having sufficient intelligence always to place the pilgrims in their correct social position. Does he make this apology to warn his readers, to entice them, or to obtain their goodwill? Why does he take so long over it? And why is he prepared to own up to lack of wit (746) but anxious to escape the charge of *vileynye* (726, 740)?

715 **in a clause** briefly.
718 Has the word *gentil* lost all sense of social superiority when it is applied to the Tabard?
719 **faste** close. There were many inns in Southwark called *The Bell*.
721 **baren us** conducted ourselves.
    ilke same.
726 **n'arette it nat** do not impute it to.
    vileynye rudeness, lack of courtesy, boorishness. *Vileynye* is the behaviour suited to a villain, or common person. It is the opposite of *gentillesse*.
731 **after a man** as someone else told it.
732 **moot reherce** must repeat. Is it true that a narrator must repeat a story as exactly as possible? Why might Chaucer want to make this claim?
733 **if it be in his charge** if it is entrusted to him.
734 However crudely (*rudeliche*) and freely (*large*) he may speak.
736 Is there something humorous in the tone here, as Chaucer explains that it would be wrong to make things up (*feyne*)?
738 'He must repeat one word as much as another' (i.e. the crude words must be included just as much as the innocent ones).
739 I cannot think of anything Christ says in the Bible which offers a precedent for the *vileynye* of some of Chaucer's language.
741 **kan hym rede** knows how to read him. Chaucer cites this remark of Plato from Boethius's (*c.* 480–524) *The Consolation of Philosophy*, which he had translated from Latin, rather than from Plato's own works (in Greek), only two of which were known in Western Europe in the fourteenth century.
742 **cosyn** closely related.
744 **Al** although, if. Do you think Chaucer is apologizing for the order of the portraits or for the action which will follow? Is he telling us that it has now become difficult to observe the niceties of social order with exactness, or that he does not wish to do so? This might reflect a more general social anxiety,

as if Chaucer recognized that in his lifetime the social status of some groups was changing and feared that this might lead him to make mistakes and become involved in quarrels.

746 Chaucer insists on his own foolishness in many of his works. Sometimes he is straightforwardly ironic, sometimes conventionally modest, and sometimes deviously denying responsibility for what he has written. Which is it here?

The Host and his proposal: Lines 747–821

Modern critical fashion is generally against attempting to discover real-life originals for the pilgrims, but most people agree that the real innkeeper Harry Baily (so named in *The Cook's Prologue*) was Chaucer's model. (See Interpretations, pages 105–106.) Harry Baily had acted as Member of Parliament for Southwark, tax-collector and coroner. There is a record of his carrying money from the Custom House to the Treasury at a time when Chaucer was Controller of Customs.

In the *General Prologue* the Host is open, merry and practical. He makes a proposal which will assure the pilgrims of an enjoyable journey and his inn of another grand feast on their return. The Host's speech is very carefully constructed in order to persuade the pilgrims to agree to his plan. First, he praises the assembled company, suggesting that he wants to repay them for their happiness with a plan that will increase their enjoyment. He is careful to emphasize that it will cost them nothing (761–8). This opening is intended to establish a climate of goodwill between himself and the pilgrims. Next he reminds the pilgrims of their purpose: to visit the shrine of St Thomas and to enjoy themselves on the journey (769–72), and argues that dumb silence will not contribute to their aim. Therefore they should band together under his leadership and he will guarantee them an enjoyable time (775–82). Why does he seek their agreement in principle before going into the details of his plan?

Once they have agreed he outlines his scheme (788–801), and he concludes by reminding them that they will enjoy themselves, by insisting that he will pay his own expenses, and by warning them that whoever contests his judgement will have to pay for what they all drink on the journey (802–09). What sort of image of himself does the Host project in this speech? What do we learn about him? Who has the most to gain from the arrangement?

The Host's plan calls for two tales from each pilgrim on the way to Canterbury and two more each on the way back. This would have resulted in a collection of at least 120 tales (allowing that Chaucer miscounts and that at least one person joins the pilgrimage *en route*). In its incomplete state *The Canterbury Tales* contains 24 tales (four of them incomplete). In *The Parson's Prologue*, the Host announces that only one more tale is required to complete the project and the journey to Canterbury (implying a one-way journey and one tale each). The introductory passages to the individual tales suggest that Chaucer changed his mind about the overall plan more than once between the statement of the plan in the *General Prologue* (probably composed in the late 1380s) and his death in 1400.

747 **Greet chiere** warm welcome.
750 **wel to drynke us leste** we were very pleased to drink.
751 **semely** suitable.
752 **marchal** master of ceremonies.
753 **eyen stepe** bright (or large) eyes.
754 **Chepe** Cheapside, one of the main streets of medieval London.
756 What is the point of saying that the Host lacked nothing in manliness (*manhod*)? (Compare with line 167.)
760 'When we had paid our bills' (the night before leaving). Perhaps there is some implication that the Host wants to assure himself that the company really is sufficiently wealthy before explaining his idea. He is practical as well as welcoming.
763 **by my trouthe** by my faith.

766 **Fayn** gladly.
　　doon yow myrthe make you merry.
767 **I am... bythoght** I have thought of.
768 Why does the Host say that his plan will cost them nothing?
769 **God yow speede** may God give you success.
770 May the heavenly martyr give you your reward!
772 **shapen yow** intend.
　　talen tell stories.
778 To abide by my decision.
779 **werken** do.
782 If you don't enjoy yourselves you may strike off my head!
784 **conseil** decision.
785 **make it wys** raise difficulties. Is Chaucer suggesting that
　　there was anything wrong with the way they agreed?
786 **graunted hym** agreed to his proposal.
787 **voirdit** verdict.
　　as hym leste as it pleased him.
789 But do not be indignant, I ask you.
791 **to shorte with** in order to shorten.
798 The most instructive and enjoyable tales.
799 **oure aller cost** all of our expense.
804 **Right... cost** entirely at my own expense.
805 **withseye** contest.
807 **vouche sauf** agree.
809 **shape me** prepare myself.
814 **reportour** record keeper.
816 **at his devys** according to his wishes.
817 **In heigh and lough** in all matters.
819 The wine was fetched (*fet*) in order to seal the agreement.

The pilgrims set out: Lines 822–858

In the morning Harry Baily asserts the authority which the pilgrims have agreed to give him. He reminds them of the penalty for disobeying his command and announces the beginning of the competition. Rather than choose the first storyteller himself, he organizes a lottery. By chance, destiny, or the manoeuvrings of the Host, the Knight draws the short straw and is chosen to tell the first story. What do we learn about the Host and the Knight from their exchange? What do we learn about the other pilgrims from their reaction?

823 **aller cok**   rooster for us all.
824 What is the implication of calling the pilgrims a flock?
825 **a litel… paas**   just above walking speed.
826 **the Wateryng of Seint Thomas**   a stream where the horses could drink, two miles along the road to Canterbury.
830 If you will stand by last night's words.
835 **ferrer twynne**   go further.
840 **lat be**   leave off.
    shamefastnesse   modesty.
841 **studieth**   deliberate, brood (with a pun for the Clerk).
844 **aventure… sort… cas**   Does the use of three such closely related words (roughly: chance, luck or destiny) indicate that the Host fixed the draw so that the Knight would start? Is there other evidence?
847 **resoun**   reasonable.
849 **what… mo?**   what more is there to say?
851 Why does Chaucer emphasize the Knight's modest acceptance? Is he making a statement about the society formed by the pilgrims? Is the Knight reluctant to begin? Is it an example of his politeness?

Interpretations

Genre, sources and background

A poem based on the telling of stories

As explained at the start of the Notes (page 33), the *General Prologue* is the first part of a large poem, the final work in Chaucer's career. He was in his mid-forties when he began *The Canterbury Tales*, an unfinished work, and the *General Prologue* is a kind of introduction to it. Using a series of personal portraits, Chaucer describes with irony, humour and sometimes criticism the people assembled for the pilgrimage to Canterbury. Whether or not he intended it, the result is the description of a cross-section of types of people drawn from a variety of ranks of medieval society. He proves to be expert in understanding the natures and dispositions of these characters assembled in the Tabard in Southwark.

After the descriptions, the storytelling challenge is put forward by the Host, a man by the name of Harry Baily, although his name is not actually made known until much later (see Notes, page 85). The challenge he sets in the *General Prologue* (788–809) is a device which establishes the well-known form and structure of *The Canterbury Tales*. The larger poem is a series of stories drawn from a number of sources and traditions which, we are asked to imagine, are each told by one of the pilgrims, most of whom are the characters described in the *General Prologue*.

But there is another important element to the whole poem which both makes it unique and continues the style started in the *General Prologue*. This element is the role that Chaucer assigns to himself as a narrator. Although each story can be enjoyed as a tale in its own right – and many of them, such as the Pardoner's, the Nun's Priest's and the Miller's have become celebrated works of literature – many are linked, providing also a story of the journey to Canterbury. Chaucer himself narrates this, often through reports of conversations, invitations, even arguments and squabbles among the band of pilgrims. In many ways it is sensible to study the *General Prologue* before the tales themselves as this helps to set the scene and context in which the tales are introduced, received and judged.

It should not come as a great surprise that Chaucer wanted to write a poem based on the telling of stories. In earlier works he appears fascinated by collections of stories. He had written a number of earlier poems, including dream-poems in which he, the narrator, was the dreamer; in *Troilus and Criseyde* he appears, rather like a novelist of later centuries, to be reading the story rather than telling it; and in *The Legend of Good Women* he sees the God of Love as an apparition who forces him to compile a variety of stories about women who died as martyrs to the cause of love. In each of these cases Chaucer – the person, the scholar and the poet – takes a role in the works while at the same time standing back from what is happening.

A similar narrative technique occurs in the *General Prologue*. Remember that Chaucer is one of the pilgrims. He says that he is *Redy to wenden on my pilgrymage* (21).

Activity

Analyse the impact of three key moments in the poem when Chaucer intervenes to make a personal comment. In what ways does he make his comments, and how does this feature help you understand the genre of the poem?

Discussion

He has turned up at the Tabard before the start of the journey to Canterbury, just like all the other pilgrims whom he describes. As a pilgrim he rather merges into the background, taking a role as a spectator/commentator which gives him a lot of flexibility. He can appear to be describing his fellow pilgrims in meticulous, factual detail, whereas in fact he might be ironically pointing out their shortcomings or eccentricities. Sometimes this is very subtle. For example, at the end of the portrait of the Merchant he informs the reader that he does not know the Merchant's name (*I noot how men hym calle*, 284). On the surface that appears to be a statement of fact, but when linked to the previous line, the irony is unmistakeable: *For sothe he was a worthy man with alle* (283).

Similarly, we might be prompted to think of the Cook in a particular way when, following a long description of his skills in the kitchen, Chaucer subtly undermines him by drawing attention to an ulcer on his shin, even though he approaches the disfigurement in a pitying tone:

> But greet harm was it, as it thoughte me,
> That on his shyne a mormal hadde he.   (385–386)

The skills of the Cook are created in one of Chaucer's characteristic lists; then through personal intervention of the narrator's voice there is a telling comment at a well-chosen moment. There is a juxtaposition of the lines describing the *blankmanger* (387) and the *mormal* (386). What is suggested by the association between the ulcer and the food?

When the poem moves on to the tales themselves we notice another feature developed from his earlier works. This is the use of a variety of styles in the stories told, clearly related to the genre of each individual tale, but also, in some of them, cleverly reflecting the character of each pilgrim as it has been described in the *General Prologue*. In this way, we cannot separate the *General Prologue* from *The Canterbury Tales* – the whole work.

As mentioned in the Notes to lines 129–31 (page 47), Chaucer was clearly influenced by the French courtly poem the *Roman de la Rose*. You can compare it with the *General Prologue* by looking at the opening of the French poem in the Appendix (page 181). As we have seen, he also drew on an idea from medieval estates satire in which characters represent their class, calling or profession and are shown satirically to fall short of what might have been expected of them. The mockery was often directed at faults in their trade, class or occupation. Of course this does not apply neatly to all of the characters in the *General*

Prologue, but the genre is evident through the descriptions of a hypocritical friar, a thieving miller, a pompous lawyer (the Sergeant of the Law) and a bankrupt merchant, among others.

Activity

Choose three references to 'estates' or status which help to define the pilgrims. Consider the extent to which these pilgrims behave as they should or whether they fall short of expectations.

Discussion

These questions may point you to some relevant examples. Remember in each case to refer back to the comments on particular lines in the Notes.

- Does the description of the Knight's behaviour in lines 69–72 help to define his dignity and nobility? Is it believable?
- Although the Squire and the Yeoman are given individual portraits they are present only as two subordinates of the Knight, and the Squire is the Knight's son. What do we learn about status and traditions in a landed society from lines 99–100? Although there are no direct comments about the Yeoman's status, what do we learn from his occupation about the Knight's way of life on his land?
- Does the Friar's reluctance to deal with poor people mock his calling? (See 240–248.)
- What do we learn about people's aspirations and ambitions in a strict hierarchical society from the latter part of the description of the Franklin? (See 355–360.)
- What do we learn about precedence in local society from the description of the petulant and irritable way that the Wife of Bath is determined always to be the first worshipper at the altar in church? (See 449–452.)
- How do you assess the effects of the Reeve's additional powers and influence? Has he got above himself? (See 597–605, for example.)

You may find other examples. But remember that estates satire did not just deal with expectations about class and position in society. It also revealed flaws in the way people performed unacceptably in their occupations or callings. You will find that this becomes a common thread when looking at the poem's themes.

The influence of Chaucer's background

Whether or not the poem was intended as estates satire, there are other influences that make it distinctive. Not least of these is the way that Chaucer brings into it his own wide knowledge of the world. This expertise allows him to switch from an account of the Crusades to life in the farmyard, from sea to land, and from Church to trade. The overall effect is not just a revealing and often humorous view of his contemporary world, but also a curious kind of documentary of medieval life in England, a sort of inventory or encyclopaedia.

Geoffrey Chaucer's own varied life suggests why he might have possessed such a detailed knowledge of the world around him. (See page 1 and the Chronology on pages 163–164 for an outline of his life.)

As a wholesale wine merchant, his father was a mercantile man but the family was also a very important one, connected to the royal household. In 1357 he joined the household of the Earl and Countess of Ulster (the Earl of Ulster was Prince Lionel, third son of Edward III). He fought in the French campaign of 1359–1360, during which he was captured and ransomed. He later worked as an attendant in the court of Edward III and was Controller of Customs in the Port of London from 1374 until 1385. Although never a professional poet as such, he showed considerable interest in the works of writers such as Dante, Petrarch and Boccaccio, which he was introduced to on his visits to Italy on royal business in the 1370s.

Considering this brief account of his life and what you learn about him elsewhere, what sort of people would he have come into contact with and what do you think he would have learned about in life?

His background and work had brought him into contact with royalty, courtiers, the military, merchants and tradesmen, innkeepers and travellers. Notice too that he would have had contact with a variety of people from different classes, which would perhaps have been quite rare for a writer.

You also need to think about the period of time in which he lived. His period was a time of change, even though society was still basically a feudal one. You can read about this in the discussion of the Knight in the Notes (pages 38–39).

In spite of the Black Death – a plague which by 1350 had reduced England's population by about a third – the second half of the fourteenth century was a relatively prosperous time in the Middle Ages. A reduced labour market (caused by the high death rate in the plague) had made many peasants better off, although on the other hand many of the great landowners, including the Church, struggling to maintain and acquire accustomed wealth, resorted to oppressive and extortionate measures against their often poor and humble tenants. Notice the fear that the Reeve, who manages his lord's estate, causes among those he deals with on the land (605).

One thing that seems very important is that Chaucer may actually have witnessed some of the gruesome events of the Peasants' Revolt in 1381. Living as he did in Aldgate at the time it is quite likely that he saw the arrival of the mob, the burning down of John of Gaunt's palace and the various beheadings of local dignitaries, including the Archbishop of Canterbury. It is said that a lot of bodies were left piled high by the side of the river, near Chaucer's home.

Industry was also changing, beginning to centre on expanding urban areas (although obviously not comparable to the sprawling urban expansion of later centuries). Ports were becoming more important, partly to meet the demands of an export trade for wool. As part of the growth of the wool trade, fulling mills were built in towns and villages near rivers ('fulling' removed grease from the wool).

However, before going on to consider some of the enjoyable and informative moments in the poem which reveal Chaucer's unquestionably wide knowledge of medieval life, it is worth noting that some critics warn us against interpreting the poem simply as a 'historical record' or 'documentary'. They point to the rich overall effect of bringing together a varied collection of characters, and how the portraits set up the main purpose of the poem, which is the storytelling.

Chaucer's knowledge of the medieval world

We get only a glimpse of Geoffrey Chaucer's understanding of the developing and changing world in the *General Prologue*; he shows much more of it in the tales. It is sometimes hard to define exactly what it is that makes the documentary effect such a strong feature. Clearly the poem was never intended just to display facts and knowledge. Yet the endless detail in his worldly knowledge, along with the catalogues of facts and references, do suggest that he wanted to make the real world a key part of the poem, set alongside the idealized world which is expressed in the opening lines and which is reflected in the purpose of a pilgrimage. This is explored more fully in the sections on themes and on critical views below (pages 106 and 143).

In a typically modest tone, Chaucer hints that a full understanding of the pilgrims is within his capabilities when he says, near the beginning, that he will describe their *condicioun* (38), their *degree* (40) and their *array* (41).

Some of the most celebrated moments in the poem come from descriptions of the characters' dress, clothing or belongings. Consider the effect on our understanding of character and appearance of the Monk's love-token (*love-knotte*, 197), the Wife of Bath's lavish headcoverings (*coverchiefs ful fyne... of ground*, 453) and the pillow case (*pilwe-beer*, 694) in which the Pardoner carries his supposed relics.

Chaucer also had a wide knowledge of the work that his characters would have been doing. The Sergeant of the Law is mocked because of his pompous nature, a judgement that seems fitting for a representative of the legal profession. Chaucer clearly knows all about what lawyers do: this man has been a judge at the court of assizes, having been given a royal commission to preside there (sit in judgement) with full judicial powers. He is also a successful buyer of land; he has an extensive knowledge of all the legal cases drawn up since the days of King William, is expert himself at drawing up legal documents and knows all the statutes (written laws) by rote. In the next portrait Chaucer shows just as much knowledge about the housekeeping skills of the Franklin, just one example of his versatility.

This worldly knowledge is not confined to what is morally acceptable: Chaucer knows only too well about the questionable practices of the Miller and the Shipman, and the wiliness of the Manciple. He is just as in touch with the criminal and illicit as he is with the world of business and science.

This worldly knowledge is sometimes presented in lists or catalogues. These often have the effect of lending a realism to the description of the characters through the use of everyday objects. The Prioress feeds her small dogs *With rosted flessh, or milk and wastel-breed* (147). The Reeve looks after his lord's stock:

> His lordes sheep, his neet, his dayerye,
> His swyn, his hors, his stoor, and his pultrye   (597–598)

All are under the Reeve's control.

The effect can also be to mock the characters, especially when lists are used in an emphatically satirical mode. The Wife of Bath's impressive history of attendance on pilgrimages is listed in the same style as the Knight's crusades:

> At Rome she hadde been, and at Boloigne,
> In Galice at Seint-Jame, and at Coloigne.   (465–466)

But we soon learn that this apparent devotion may have been for dubious reasons, perhaps to attract husbands. Likewise the Summoner's scabrous skin complaints cannot be cured by any substance available in medicine:

Ther nas quyk-silver, lytarge, ne brymstoon,
Boras, ceruce, ne oille of tartre noon... (629–630)

One other point to consider is this: does the constant use of lists displaying such wide general knowledge contribute to the characterization of Chaucer himself, perhaps establishing the cleverness of the poet?

Activity

Choose one or more of these areas of Chaucer's general knowledge and show what he knew of the subject: astronomy and medicine (e.g. the Doctor of Physic); cookery (e.g. the Cook, the Franklin); geography (e.g. the Merchant, the Shipman); working on the land (e.g. the Yeoman, the Ploughman, the Reeve). About which other subjects did he have a strong general knowledge?

What, in your view, does realism contribute to the poem?

Discussion

It is important to try to understand the place of realism in the poem, and not to exaggerate the importance of the 'documentary' effect. In fact, Chaucer's desire to root the poem so firmly in the world of everyday life may have had a much more important purpose than simply to document medieval society. Compare the realism with the idealized opening. What are the effects of the contrasting tones?

The realism in the *General Prologue* can be contrasted with an idealized view of life which was drawn from the style and arrangement of French courtly literature. This often had a very static, polite, pure and formal tone. Most commentators and critics emphasize the fact that in the poem Chaucer's world is a very real place. He did use a developing realistic tradition of medieval literature in which he would have learned to characterize his people in a more down-to-earth style using domestic descriptions and imagery in familiar settings, along with colloquial and even impolite terms. But critics also point to hints of a contrasting, idealized world. The opening lines have an elevated style with a vision of universal change and rebirth, suggesting a powerful central theme of regeneration.

The lines that describe the intentions of the characters assembling at the Tabard in early spring suggest that they should have a strongly devout purpose (see Notes, page 35):

> from every shires ende
> Of Engelond to Caunterbury they wende,
> The hooly blisful martir for to seke,
> That hem hath holpen whan that they were seeke.   (15–18)

But in fact the kind of piety we might expect to find in pilgrims travelling to give thanks at the shrine of St Thomas à Becket seems notably lacking, apart from in the Knight, the Parson and the Ploughman. What is the effect of placing these three idealized characters alongside others who are morally less correct, and some downright immoral?

What might Chaucer have been trying to achieve by including so much realism in a poem about such a holy activity, and basing the characters – or at least many of them – so firmly in their daily comings and goings? These are some of the questions that critics have raised about this tension:

- Was he undermining the purpose of pilgrimage?
- Was he exposing the more corrupt side of human beings?
- Was he even celebrating and rejoicing in the way that people lived their lives – full of energy, personal motivation and strong individual desires?

Form and structure

The portraits of the pilgrims take up most of the poem. However, the overall form and structure of the work depend also on the opening and the ending. These sections will now be considered in order to support interpretations of the poem as a whole, which can sometimes appear complex. Three aspects will be discussed: the messages and possible meanings of the opening lines; the voice, role and character of Chaucer himself; and the storytelling challenge issued by the Host at the end of the poem.

The messages in the opening lines

Before introducing the pilgrims, Chaucer begins the *General Prologue* with 42 opening lines which appear to set a tone for some of the meanings in the poem as a whole. Their true importance and their potential spiritual and worldly meanings have been the subject of a great deal of debate and discussion by Chaucer critics (see pages 145–146).

A world undergoing its rebirth in spring is celebrated. The language is uplifting and enthusiastic. Look at how the sheer sensuous energy is established through the personification of the months of March and April, the latter month having:

> bathed every veyne in swich licour
> Of which vertu engendred is the flour   (3–4)

Then look at the vivid way that:

> Zephirus eek with his sweete breeth
> Inspired hath in every holt and heeth
> The tendre croppes   (5–7)

In the Notes on pages 34–36 there is a detailed description of some of the tensions in the opening sentence, most prominently the tension between the awakening of sexual love (see in particular the note about *corages* in line 11) and the spiritual devotion expected of pilgrims. Some interpretations of the opening lines have seen more explicit sexual symbolism based on the personification of the two months of spring, suggesting the impregnating of a female March by a male April, and the marriage of earth and water.

This traditional opening with its partly elevated style is exciting and uplifting, immediately establishing a theme of rebirth and regeneration through the forces of the natural world.

April from *Les Très Riches Heures du Duc de Berry*. Compare this image with the descriptions of spring in lines 1–18 and Appendix, page 181.

There is then very quickly a contrast with the more realistic description of preparation for a pilgrimage, in the Tabard, in South London. From the universally significant realms of seasonal, cosmic and natural life, then to the yearning for foreign pilgrimages engendered in such an inspiring new season, Chaucer soon brings the reader's focus right down to earth:

> Bifil that in that seson on a day,
> In Southwerk at the Tabard as I lay...   (19–20)

What is the effect of this sudden change of style? It seems curious that, following such an elevated opening, there should be a marked difference in style, switching to a more chatty, anecdotal and familiar kind of language, which seems out of place when compared to the style of the first 11 lines. It is also worth pausing for thought on the possible connections between the sensuous opening and the purposes of medieval pilgrimage. These may not appear automatically linked. Many critics analysing the opening have suggested that there is indeed a connection between the energy of nature as it is presented (the climax being the nightingale's nocturnal incitement of spirit) and the enthusiasm for indulgence of one sort or another which was beginning to characterize late medieval pilgrimages.

The emphasis during the description of spring is most definitely on the creativity and energy of the season, but this is surely idealized with sensuous exaggeration. Given the contradiction in the suggestion that March is a dry month in England and also the classical presence of *Zephirus*, a god bringing freshness to the world on the mild west wind, this part of the poem seems utterly unreal. While there are elements of realism (the *holt and heeth*, the *tendre croppes* and the *smale foweles*) the effect is that, in spite of the poem's realistic setting in the Tabard, with pilgrim travellers preparing for their journey, the opening is quite the opposite – classical, idealized, romantic, unearthly.

Chaucer's role in the poem

The idealized description of spring gives way to a realistic description of English pilgrimages:

> And specially from every shires ende
> Of Engelond to Caunterbury they wende   (15–16)

This is followed by the presence of Chaucer's own voice in the description of what is happening in the Tabard as he prepares to make his own pilgrimage along with his 29 companions (see Note to line 24, page 37), whom, while he has *tyme and space* (35) he will describe. When in lines 19 and 20 we first become aware of Chaucer's own voice in the poem, we may miss some of the significance. From the nineteenth century onwards we are used to the first-person narrator in novels and even in poems, but the difference is that in these cases the narrator is usually a character who just happens to be telling the story. In *The Canterbury Tales* the 'character' (a pilgrim who is a poet) is also the writer. It is perhaps most similar to what we think of as autobiography, although with one main difference – as far as we know, the night in Southwark and the journey and tales that follow are fictional experiences.

The arrangement makes for an interesting interpretation of the narrative structure. Whose voice is really the narrator's? Is it Chaucer as the writer or as the poet/pilgrim? That's the limit of the quandary in the *General Prologue*, but when the tales themselves are told later in the poem, the matter becomes further complicated, as of course the tales are each 'told' by a pilgrim, with Chaucer intervening, if at all, only at the beginning and end of each story. So who tells the tales? Is it the pilgrims, is it Chaucer the poet/pilgrim who has heard them, or is it Chaucer the writer who of course masterminds the whole thing? Can you see how there is a type of narrative displacement in the form? Let us go on to explore some of the possible purposes and effects.

In his apology which comes at the end of the portraits (715–746) he appears to deny all responsibility for his language and the content of the tales he will tell, and he wishes to be judged humbly, although there may be a deliberate self-consciousness in this position. He also curiously puts himself down: *My wit is short, ye may wel understonde* (746).

Can we accept all this humility at face value, or do you think there is a kind of mischief in his words? Earlier, he stated that while he considered it important to describe the appearance of the pilgrims, this would be *so as it semed me* (39). As a result, are we to believe his descriptions, accepting them as the simple truth, or should we take them with a pinch of salt? Does drawing attention to his (declared) shortcomings enhance or diminish his credibility as a faithful reporter?

Within the apology there are other features in his language which cast light on his character as a poet. For one thing, if he is to relay the tales as they are spoken, in the interests of truth this will include language *rudeliche and large* (734), as it will be spoken by the various story-tellers.

Is this all just politeness, or is there a cleverly constructed pose? Part of the purpose of his false modesty may be to make him appear less responsible for what is said. Some of the tales are quite 'bawdy', with sexual jokes and blasphemous language. To what extent is his reserve just a tactic?

Chaucer, presumably as the pilgrim, soon expresses a wish to be thought of as one of the company. He is quickly *of hir felaweshipe anon* (32). Neither the structure of the poem, nor perhaps his own modesty, allow for a comparable style of portrait of the poet. However, he is able, subtly and with an apparent lack of self-consciousness, to reveal his own character. Of course, there is none of the minute detail of appearance, physique or history that we get with the other pilgrims, but there are just enough glimpses of the image he has of his own skills, and occasional expressions of opinion, sometimes even colluding with the failings of fellow pilgrims, for example about the Monk: *And I seyde his opinion was good* (183).

There is also a strong impression of his intelligence and perceptiveness, and an emerging indication of his moral code and philosophy, which seems tolerant of harmless frailties but severe against those who mean to harm and cheat others. Can we also find a superior air in him when he passes comment, as he does in the above reference to the Monk's attitudes? He can be very dismissive, as with the anonymity of the Merchant and his mockery of the preoccupations of the Sergeant of the Law. What conclusion can you draw from his comment on the fact that the Prioress speaks French not in the fashion of the royal court but *After the scole of Stratford atte Bowe* (125)?

Activity

In the same way that the other pilgrims, or at least 26 of them, are described, try writing a portrait of Chaucer himself – the Poet. You could do this in either prose or poetry, and a challenge would be to do it in Middle English. Composing a section in Middle English would be a good way of helping you to understand how the language works.

Discussion

It will be difficult to include a physical description of Chaucer, although there is a portrait of him on page 3. You should be able to find evidence of his outlook on life in order to make an assessment of his character, and of course you know something about his varied biography.

He appears to be conscious of social status, although you will need to ask yourself whether he would respect people of high status if they displayed faults. We have repeatedly discovered him to be worldly, knowledgeable and even learned, which sometimes encourages him to a degree of showiness, such as through his exhaustive lists and categories of general knowledge and gleaned facts. But should this be a fault in a man whose profession is words? Clearly worldliness, through his extensive travel and his mercantile background, have stood him in good stead as a writer. He is well informed, even if prone to exaggeration, about the Knight's crusades in areas of the Mediterranean and eastern Europe, and equally at ease with merchant voyages as he describes the Europe of the Shipman.

He appears to be able to laugh gently at the less harmful failings in human beings and ridicule those that exert a more dangerous influence. He certainly has the ability to detect and expose corruption, and seems particularly critical of material greed and avarice, especially when harm is done to others. What will you want to say about his sense of humour?

Perhaps above all, Geoffrey Chaucer comes across as an enthusiast. He admires the abundant qualities through which his fellow human beings show their love of life. In this respect, what does he admire (sometimes in spite of their faults) in the Squire, the Monk, the Franklin, the Yeoman, the Shipman, the Doctor of Physic, the Prioress and the Wife of Bath?

He appears fascinated by the inherent quality in the approaches to life of the Knight, the Parson and the Ploughman; and he has an envious appreciation of the opportunism and *joie de vivre* of the

Host. All of these outlooks may contrast with his expression of the negative forces in the Reeve, the Summoner and the Pardoner.

Elsewhere, admittedly, he may have had to pass quickly over the avarice of the Friar, the hypocrisy of the Merchant, the temper of the Franklin and the crimes of the Shipman and Miller, but in reality none of their failings are as despised as those which belong to the last trio: a Reeve whose cunning and insect-like features repulse people; a Summoner whose scaly physical appearance is matched only by the slippery ignorance of his frightening behaviour; and finally the Pardoner, who may be the cleverest of his kind but is intentionally a swindler. What do these lines tell us about *Chaucer*?

> But of his craft, fro Berwyk into Ware
> Ne was ther swich another pardoner. (692–693)

As you write the portrait, don't forget to imagine his horse, how he rode it and in what position in the group.

The Host's challenge

The Tabard, with its roomy chambers and stables, was likely to have been a superior inn. The Host would have been responsible for the conduct of all guests under his roof; he would have had to remove their weapons for safekeeping and ensure that they did not venture out after curfew; there would have been restrictions on the food and drink he could make on the premises, and he would have been restricted with fixed charges on his tariff.

We could be led to imagine that many of the more indulgent characters spent their entire evening in the Tabard eating and drinking. They were being well looked after by the hospitable Harry Baily (his name is revealed in *The Cook's Prologue*). There is a cheery atmosphere, aided by strong wine: *Strong was the wyn, and wel to drynke us leste* (750).

The Host's character is expressed through his dialogue and actions, and there is only a brief account of the man, who resembles in some ways the Monk, the Franklin and the Guildsmen:

> A large man he was with eyen stepe –
> A fairer burgeys was ther noon in Chepe –
> Boold of his speche, and wys, and wel ytaught,
> And of manhod hym lakkede right naught. (753–756)

This perceptiveness, manliness and worldly wisdom are soon, as we see from his challenge, to be turned to opportunism. He has fed the company well and they have drunk strong wine. He then appears to have little difficulty persuading the pilgrims – effectively his customers – to agree to his proposal. As has been suggested in the Notes (pages 85–86) he will be assured of another night's business, although of course this never happens in the poem as a whole.

We come to learn more about this genial character during the interludes between the tales themselves, as he often acts as a kind of master of ceremonies, orchestrating the storytelling with careful control, intervening in squabbles and keeping everybody happy. It is often easy to suspend our disbelief and feel that the story of the pilgrimage is really happening. This is partly because of the apparent realism created through the dialogues with the Host. However, just as we wonder about Chaucer's role, we need to remember that the Host is another character constructed by Chaucer, a literary device, and one whom, again, Chaucer can hide behind. The storytelling competition is not Chaucer's (the pilgrim's) idea, but the Host's, and it is not Chaucer who is distracting the other pilgrims from devotion.

The opening lines, the unusual role of the narrator and the Host's challenge all contribute to a complexity in the form of the poem.

Themes and subject matter

Within the overall structure of the poem we find themes of rebirth and energy, but because a large part of the poem is the sequence of portraits of the pilgrims, inevitably many of the subjects and themes arise out of the descriptions of the *sondry folk… In felaweshipe* (25–26). Below, there is exploration of some of the main impressions of medieval society, but remember it is not really possible to separate the themes from the characters. What we learn about life in medieval times is evident from the portraits. In the section on characterization (see pages 128–133) there is a discussion about the relationship between the characters as individuals and as types of people, with their character and appearance dictated by their professions or roles in life.

The age of chivalry

In the golden age of chivalry, medieval knights exemplified the very ideals of chivalric behaviour and morals. The strength of the Order of Knighthood lay not so much in its numbers as in the acceptance of its ideals, and the evidence is that medieval people certainly believed in these ideals. See the comment in the Notes (page 39) on lines 45–46, where Chaucer sets out the qualities in his *parfit gentil knyght* (72).

Chivalry, in the late Middle Ages, suggested a religious, social and moral code as well as military prowess. In his account of the Knight, Chaucer complements the idealistic abstractions of *chivalrie,/ Trouthe… honour, fredom and curteisie* (45–46) by a series of powerful intensifying adjectives and adverbs which stress the Knight's abundant goodness and recognize his idealized character, his standing and role in life:

> Ful worthy was he in his lordes werre,
> And therto hadde he riden, no man ferre,
> As wel in cristendom as in hethenesse   (47–49)

Do you think the description makes him appear more as an idealized type – of knights in general – or as a real person? Although the overall quality of his perfect character may be hard to believe, it has been suggested that he may have been based on a real man who, as a contemporary and acquaintance

The illustration of the Knight from the Ellesmere manuscript

of Chaucer's, would have taken part in the series of crusades listed.

As well as establishing his worthiness through a description of his character, Chaucer notes the Knight's military pedigree with an impressive list of the battles he has fought in the Crusades, stressing the practical application to which he has courageously put his Christian values. The only note of realism comes at the end of the portrait with a few details of his modest appearance and the information that he has joined the pilgrimage with no time to change his armour, as he has just returned from a campaign abroad. (Does this seem far fetched?) The realism contributes to the chivalry, with his tunic stained by the rust from his coat of mail.

The themes of honour and chivalry are extended in an appropriately hierarchical manner in the portraits of the Knight's son, the young Squire, and their servant the Yeoman.

SQUIRE.

The illustration of the Squire from the Ellesmere manuscript

Activity

Go through the first two descriptions, of the Knight and the Squire. Re-read the sections from the Notes on each of these pilgrims.

What evidence of chivalry in the Middle Ages do you find in their portraits?

Discussion

The word *chivalry* effectively meant a *warrior on horseback*, but it came to mean a lot more; it was a generic term for strong virtues and qualities in men who fought bravely against infidels and who would honour and serve their king and God. They should do nothing to displease ladies. Like monks they had to take vows, regulating their activity and behaviour. They would spend many years as squires serving their masters, practising the art of war.

Clearly you will wish to consider the list of the Knight's campaigns, suggesting as they do from lines 51–66 that he has ridden out and been immensely successful in defeating 'heathens' in

Mediterranean Muslim lands and islands, as well as in the eastern parts of Europe. The Notes (page 40) indicate that the list is a fairly random selection of campaigns and battles, possibly reinforcing the idea that this is an idealized general description of a knight rather than a portrait of a particular man. His chivalrous activity and high standing are not only indicated through his military accomplishments but also through the fact that he has been highly honoured: *Ful ofte tyme he hadde the bord bigonne* (52) and through his humble, submissive and innocent mode of behaving.

It is understandable that his son, the Squire, is youthful and amorous – he is only 20 years of age – but his honour and nobility shine through in the description from line 85 of his early successes as a young soldier, which he hopes will stand him *in his lady grace* (88). Notice also the ritual described in the final line of his portrait.

Materialism in the secular (non-religious) world

The following descriptions of London in Chaucer's time are intended to show how he lived in a society that was increasingly marked out by economic growth. In other words money and trade were becoming more important. Along with economic growth came greed, materialism and, inevitably, poverty and squalor. In another section of these Interpretations (pages 114–118), we look at how this money-grabbing instinct had affected the Church, but for the moment the emphasis is on the descriptions of the secular world of trade and industry, and their effects on medieval life.

> Chaucer's world was complex. London, the focal point, was a place of paradox [contradictions]: it resounded with the construction of churches and palaces proclaiming the glory of God and of man; it was the arena for ruthless political manoeuvres, bitter trade dissentions and widescale suffering caused by inhumanity, poverty and disease.
>
> (Clair C. Olson, 'Chaucer and Fourteenth-Century Society' in *A Companion to Chaucer Studies*, ed. Beryl Rowland, Oxford University Press, p. 32)

London was in a class of its own: the only medieval town with a population probably in excess of 50,000 in the late fourteenth century. It was an entrepot for the kingdom, a terminal of the Baltic, North Sea and Mediterranean trades: it attracted immigrants from the Home Counties and East Anglia, and especially from the East Midlands; and its suburbs were creeping up towards Westminster. No less than in the countryside these changes unsettled life in a number of towns, whose burgess oligarchies strove to maintain their control in a changing world. The landowners of England thus strove to counter the economic crisis, but it was often at the price of straining relations with an increasingly assertive peasantry and established urban communities.

(Ralph Griffiths, *The Oxford Illustrated History of Britain*, ed. K.O. Morgan, p. 190)

No period of history is ever characterized by one mood. Like many other periods of change, the late fourteenth century was a varied one. However, there was a marked growth in economic life and this may have been accompanied by avarice (greed) and materialism, which certainly Chaucer reflects in the characteristics of a number of the pilgrims.

In several of the portraits of the characters who were involved in this new economic life, we see how a love of money and the lifestyles associated with wealth are strong factors motivating the behaviour of a new and emerging class of men in an increasingly urban world. The Guildsmen, the Merchant, the Doctor of Physic and the Manciple reflect this new world. Connections between a love of profit and other character traits arise in ironic and amusing ways. The Merchant's elegant and neat appearance, his bearing on his horse and his rather pompous obsession with stating the value of his profits all conceal the possibility that he may be heavily in debt. His operations in a money market show that he is involved in the beginnings of a capitalist money-lending system. (See Notes, page 55.) Success could bring great wealth and social esteem, but these were activities fraught with danger, and the risks of bankruptcy were high. Do you find a contrast between his elegant appearance and proud bearing and his rather shaky financial circumstances?

The ironic dismissal of this self-important merchant – *But, sooth to seyn, I noot how men hym calle* (284) – suggests this tension between success and failure. He is undermined by his anonymity.

A similar thing happens in the portrait of the Sergeant of the Law. He too gives an impression of influential activity in his business as a purchaser of land. He is a character of considerable standing and qualities, having been appointed by the king to be a Justice of the Peace. He is dignified in appearance and respected for his knowledge. Chaucer uses hyperboles to describe his work: there is nobody more successful at buying land; his written contracts are faultless; there are no problems or half measures in the land purchases he has made – *Al was fee symple to hym in effect* (319).

However, like the Merchant, he is also cut down to size as Chaucer remarks that he *semed bisier than he was* (322).

The pride of the Guildsmen, all of whom possess both property and income, is partly given expression through the ambitiousness of their wives, for whom it would be *ful fair to been ycleped 'madame'* (376) should their husbands aspire to the office of aldermen. See also the Note to lines 371–372 (page 62), hinting that their 'wisdom' may have been spoken consciously to advance their own cause.

In other descriptions there is a connection between the profit motive and personality. There is a clear hint that the Shipman lacks a conscience, and in the course of his trade is a thief and pirate. (See the Note to line 400, page 64.) The style in which this rogue is portrayed is typically matter of fact, perhaps suggesting that his activities were the norm rather than the exception.

The Doctor of Physic unashamedly keeps all the money that comes his way in times of plague: *He kepte that he wan in pestilence* (442). The Miller is a clever thief and swindler – *Wel koude he stelen corn and tollen thries* (562) – and the Manciple is so clever in the dealings he has with his masters in the Inns of Court that he is able to swindle them all.

Activity

Consider carefully the group of 'mercantile-class' pilgrims – those whose work and lives revolve around money and trade. Choose one of them and explain how his financial situation and attitude towards money is conveyed. Can you find other characteristics that show links between this character's personality and his professional behaviour?

Discussion

Chaucer's capacity to see through his characters and to reveal their basic motives is never more strong than when he describes those affected by the profit motive. The power of wealth is tenacious, and to describe its hold on some of the characters he uses some strong imagery. For example, the Doctor of Physic, well practised in the science of the medieval medical profession, is given health and happiness through his delight in profit:

> For gold in phisik is a cordial,
> Therefore he lovede gold in special.   (443–444)

The Miller, a dishonest scoundrel, steals grain and takes his toll for it three times over. His love of money is brought out in a vivid metaphor: *And yet he hadde a thombe of gold, pardee* (563).

Self-importance and ambition are represented not just through imagery but by heightened realism, sometimes through the actions of the characters, or by their tone of voice and appearance. The Merchant is *Sownynge* (275) always on the subject of his transactions and profit. There is a vivid impression of the Doctor of Physic treating his patients *by his magyk natureel* (416), and the Guildsmen appear with their lavish equipment beautifully mounted and adorned (365–368).

Any age produces its barterers and traffickers, hagglers and hucksters, as well as thieves and scoundrels. In the *General Prologue* there are a few direct references to these kinds of dealings. Do we learn anything about the conscience of a smuggler when we are told that the Shipman takes no account of his enemies but unceremoniously throws them overboard in a fight? And does the daunting appearance of the Miller make it more or less surprising that he should steal corn?

The self-image of some of the other characters may mean that they think of themselves as upright and important members of society. However, there are hints and revelations that they have become wholly affected by the prospects of profit and social advance. This can happen through chance comments, which may need a second glance before their full importance is revealed. What significance is there in the way the Merchant wears his boots (273), the Guildsmen their apparel (365–368) and the Doctor of Physic his colourful coat (439–440)? What might Chaucer have been suggesting when he says that the Doctor *knew the cause of everich maladye* (419)? Does this mean that he really did know the cause of each illness, or that he claimed he did?

Even if Chaucer seems at times economical with the truth about the financial dealings of some of these characters, there are often hints in their appearance and general behaviour to suggest avarice and pomposity. However, it is not untypical of Chaucer to appear just a little wary of revealing the full truth about dishonest dealings. Why might this have been the case?

In many ways of course, avarice, greed and the profit motive are revealed more explicitly through the descriptions of some of the characters representing the Church, a theme explored in the next section.

The Church

At times the poem suggests that the officials of the Church were driven almost entirely by greed and a love of money. The two descriptions of the Parson and the Ploughman contrast directly with other Church characters, the contrast highlighting the overall corruption in the others. These two characters are models of frugal behaviour, driven only by a desire to please God. But they seem to be idealized characters, adding to the impression that they are presented primarily as a means of highlighting the materialism and worldliness of the other ecclesiastical pilgrims. The Parson exhibits humble generosity, a trait which is the opposite of any profit motive:

> But rather wolde he yeven, out of doute,
> Unto his povre parisshens aboute
> Of his offryng and eek of his substaunce.   (487–489)

And his Ploughman brother works on the land:

> For Cristes sake, for every povre wight,
> Withouten hire, if it lay in his myght.   (537–538)

These two singular examples are contrasted with a succession of materialistic and self-indulgent approaches to life from nearly all the other Church characters. The Friar most resembles the mercantile characters in his efforts to achieve social status: he would prefer to keep company with innkeepers, barmaids and local merchants of victuals, rather than lower himself in the eyes of the community through association with lepers and beggars.

PARSON.

The illustration of the Parson from the Ellesmere manuscript

Activity

There is evidence of greed and the profit motive among four characters from the Church. Show how this failing is brought out in the description of either the Monk or the Friar.

Discussion

Any criticism or mockery of the Monk and the Friar is less severe than the treatment of the Summoner and the Pardoner. The Monk, for example, is treated with mild irony rather than harsh criticism. His clothes alone suggest that he must be well off. The Friar is described as *a wantowne and a merye* (208), clearly not a style of life appropriate for a man who should have devoted himself to the rules of his religious order. Yet this sort of comment is mild in tone compared to many of the lines used later about the Summoner and the Pardoner.

Notice the energy and enthusiasm in the description of the Monk; it is one of the more colourful and vibrant descriptions. He is brought to life as someone who loves everything that life has to offer, far more interested in riding, hunting and eating well than he is in religious study:

> What sholde he studie and make hymselven wood,
> Upon a book in cloystre alwey to poure...?   (184–185)

What are their real motives for performing their ecclesiastical duties to such perfection? Consider the Monk's clothing (193–197). Why is the Friar's *'In principio'* (254) so pleasant? What is Chaucer implying about the Friar through the use of a proverbial phrase in line 256? (See Notes, page 54.)

Evidence of avarice in the Church

How typical was this taste for wealth and well-being in the medieval Church? Muriel Bowden, in *A Commentary on the General Prologue to The Canterbury Tales* (see Further Reading), has discovered numerous references to the state of avaricious hypocrisy among contemporaries of Chaucer's characters. She quotes from John Gower, another medieval writer, who complained of monks in his *Mirour de l'Omme*:

> The monk of the present day wears a habit which is a beautiful adornment to the body, and for vain honour he is clad in a furred cloak. Let the monk be filled with consternation who makes himself handsome for the world, who wears the finest wool furred with costly grey squirrel rather than a hair shirt!

Here is another revealing quotation from Thomas Wright's collection of medieval *Political Poems and Songs*. An honest ploughman has this to say about monks he knows:

> Some wearen mitre and ring,
> With double worsted well ydight,
> With royall meat and rich drinke,
> And rideth on a courser as a knight.

Gower, a much more orthodox Christian than Geoffrey Chaucer, wrote of the Franciscan Order:

> The Friars preach of poverty yet they always have an open hand to receive riches. They have perverted their Order from within by their covetousness. They wish ease, but they will not labour – in no case do they do their duty.

Summoners were regularly attacked in political poems, often out of contempt for the way they did the business of avaricious bishops or archdeacons who, again in Wright's words, 'cared for neither right nor wrong if they smell a bribe'. In fact the extortionate behaviour of summoners was the subject of a parliamentary plea, dated 1378. In this plea they were accused of harassing poor people going out to work in the fields and forcing their victims to attend courts (see Notes, page 77) a long way from their own homes, thus making them even more poor. In the plea there was a conclusion that summoners were causing:

> great dis-ease, impoverishment, and oppression of the said poor Commons. It is begged that Parliament consider these great harms.

The Church contributed directly to the potential for dishonesty among pardoners. These were often vagabonds rather than the genuine churchmen who would have been authorized to buy and sell relics from Rome in order to offer redemption and salvation to sinners who repented and confessed. The practice was invariably corrupt: indulgences were forged and pardons were sold without any question of a proper confession. The Pope himself, Boniface IX – aware of the widespread malpractice – charged in a papal edict of 1390 that henceforth all pardoners be made to vow that they came fully authorized from Rome.

Other failings in the characters from the Church

The characters connected with the Church have other failings as well as materialism and greed, although the profit motive does appear to be at the heart of the breakdown in its moral authority.

No group of characters more fully represents the contrast in the poem between the expectations of a calling and the reality of life. In other words, the pilgrims are too often not what they should have been. From the descriptions of the very pilgrims whose vocations should have been devout responses to their holy duties, we gain instead an impression of worldliness, self-indulgence and corruption. As a large landowner, the Church was involved in daily dealings with the mass of people whose lives and well-being depended on how well they were treated. Increasingly, the financial and legal affairs of Church officials were routine activities as important as the pastoral ones.

Because it was a landowner and as a result of long-established practice, the Church required people to pay tithes. These were a tax paid to the Church by all its local parishioners. It also made money in other ways and, as we see clearly in the practices of the

Summoner, undertook judicial tasks, such as the summoning of offenders, both moral and secular, to court.

Chaucer's description of the Parson expresses how, ideally, the duties of the Church should have been carried out. He is a diligent parish priest who tramps in all weathers on foot about his entire parish, his staff symbolically held in his hand. He genuinely lives by the law of Christ *and his apostles twelve* (527), and he exemplifies in his own personal devotion to high moral standards the values he expects in others. But he is unique. His literal obedience of Christ's law contrasts with the hypocrisy of many of the other characters, although that is not to say that Chaucer necessarily condemns them all.

Some of the worldliness and personal vitality in the Monk and the Friar are qualities Chaucer even seems to admire. He is also conscious of the considerable clerical and secular skills possessed by some of the churchmen, even when they are behaving hypocritically. Much of this element of the descriptions is expressed ironically. What is he suggesting when he tells us, for example, of the Friar that *plesaunt was his absolucioun* (222), and that the Pardoner was a *noble ecclesiaste* (708)?

There is an ambiguous view of the Monk – *a fair for the maistrie* (165). He warms to his philosophy of abandoning the old Benedictine rule as too restrictive. On the other hand, his love of hunting and sport, activities which may have been disloyal to the orders of his monastery, and his wealth and elaborate appearance make him more worldly than spiritual. But how harsh is Chaucer's tone? Are there things about the Monk that Chaucer admires?

The Friar is exposed as a greater hypocrite. How skilful are his deceptions? He has considerable powers of language, is gratifying in confession and graciously humble when it most suits him. In the same way that the Pardoner is ironically described as a *noble ecclesiaste* (708), the Friar is a *worthy lymytour* (269) – he is licensed to beg for his order.

Some critics have noted the sheer vitality in the characters of the pilgrims, even if some of the things they do are questionable morally. This theme of human vitality is apparent in the Monk and the Friar, especially when they are compared with the Clerk, whose austerity (the opposite of indulgence) is described rather pitifully:

> And he nas nat right fat, I undertake,
> But looked holwe, and therto sobrely.　　　　　(288–289)

The Clerk may be a man who genuinely prays for the souls of his benefactors, but he presents to the world an aloof and unexciting appearance which Chaucer hardly admires. The Clerk has the works of Aristotle, for learned reference and inspiration, at the head of his bed. This contrasts strikingly with the Monk, who:

> yaf nat of that text a pulled hen,
> That seith that hunters ben nat hooly men,
> Ne that a monk, whan he is recchelees,
> Is likned til a fissh that is waterlees　　　　(177–180)

Are similar comparisons possible between lines describing the Friar and the Parson?

The Friar is exposed as hypocritical and greedy, but otherwise there appears to be little by way of condemnation in Chaucer's treatment of the first group of characters from the Church (the Prioress will be discussed later), and there are even tones of admiration.

Activity

How does the tone change for the descriptions of the Summoner and the Pardoner? What techniques does Chaucer use to reveal their characters? How do their physical characteristics and appearances add to our impressions of their immoral conduct?

Discussion

Corruption waits till the last. As if finally to assert his moral credentials, just as he started with the most noble and honourable of men, the Knight, Chaucer ends with the two most loathsome pilgrims, the Summoner and the Pardoner. The Summoner is also the most revolting physically.

Both of these characters work in readily corruptible positions. Do you think it is their offices or their personalities that Chaucer wants to expose and condemn? Look at the vivid character assassination of the Summoner. What do we learn about him in the section starting at line 635, as he is described when drunk? What do we think of someone who exhausts the extent of his learning so quickly and speaks like the mimicry of a parrot? How does his dismissal of the power of excommunication compare with the Parson's attitude to sinners (*What so he were, of heigh or lough estat*, 522)? Chaucer is unusually rude about the Summoner's appearance. Does he intend a connection between his ugly looks and his powers of corruption?

Consider the tone used to describe the Pardoner's false eloquence as a preacher. What effect would he have had on his congregations? And is there further comparison to be made with the Parson?

> Wel oghte a preest ensample for to yive,
> By his clennesse, how that his sheep sholde lyve.   (505–506)

Part of Chaucer's art lies in his capacity to express corruption in lines about personal appearance. This undoubtedly happens with the Summoner. Does the same happen with the Pardoner? What impression do you get of the Pardoner's character from the description of his apparent effeminacy and the image he has of himself riding *al of the newe jet* (682) – in the latest fashion? What might the other pilgrims have thought of the audacious way he tries to sell indulgences? Why might they have been wary of him? Is there anything at all redeeming or impressive about him?

Food, drink and greet chiere

We have already considered the role of the Host. Eating and drinking as a theme surfaces elsewhere in the poem. The vivid account of the Prioress's table manners helps to detail her flourishing courtliness:

> Hir over-lippe wyped she so clene
> That in hir coppe ther was no ferthyng sene
> Of grece, whan she dronken hadde hir draughte.
> Ful semely after hir mete she raughte.   (133–136)

The possibility is that Chaucer based these lines on a remarkably similar passage from the *Roman de la Rose* in which a woman uses her elegant and fastidious table manners to be attractive to her lover (see Appendix, pages 182–183).

The indulgent Monk, who loves hunting, is afforded one of the most succulent lines in English literature: *A fat swan loved he best of any roost* (206).

The Friar associates with franklins, preferring their genial company to that of beggars and lepers, whose plight should have consumed more of his time. We are told that his preference is to deal *al with riche and selleres of vitaille* (248).

The underfed Clerk contrasts with the more gluttonous pilgrims. This gaunt Oxford scholar is rather similar in build to his emaciated horse:

> As leene was his hors as is a rake,
> And he nas nat right fat, I undertake,
> But looked holwe, and therto sobrely.   (287–289)

Indulgence is most evident in the description of the Franklin. This successful landowner, who has been a Member of Parliament, is another of the characters who lives his life to the full, just like the Monk and the Friar. He also resembles the Wife of Bath. Like her, he is capable of losing his temper rather severely; we learn how cross he can become with his cook (351–352). His epicurean philosophy leads him to believe that *pleyn delit/ Was verray felicitee parfit* (337–338), pure pleasure being the sign of a life of perfect happiness.

FRANKLIN.

The illustration of the Franklin from the Ellesmere manuscript

---

Activity

What does Chaucer mean when he describes the Franklin as *sangwyn*? See the Note to line 333 (page 60) which explains the humours by which it was assumed that medieval people were governed.

How is the indulgent character of the Franklin established? Refer also to two other portraits to show how the theme of indulgence is developed elsewhere.

Discussion

A little understanding of medieval feasting might help you to see that characters such as the Franklin were not out of the ordinary. In contrast to the vulnerability of the poor to famine and plague, many landowners and wealthy people in the late fourteenth century were living very comfortable lives. It is clear that the Franklin arranges things so that food and drink in his household are not merely a matter of sustenance but available as a permanent feast. He has changed the earlier medieval practice of taking down the trestle table between meals, leaving it permanently in place in his hall:

> His table dormant in his halle alway
> Stood redy covered al the longe day. (353–354)

A medieval feast would have been a truly sumptuous affair. See the illustration from the Luttrell Psalter below. Muriel Bowden, in *A Commentary on the General Prologue to The Canterbury Tales* (see Further Reading), lists a first course of brawn with mustard, bacon and peas; beef and boiled chickens (boiling was a popular way of cooking meat in the Middle Ages); roast goose, capon, and a richly made dish of pastries stuffed with cream, eggs, vegetables, fruit and spices. This would invariably have been followed by a rich stew of meat or fish and more stuffed pastries; then thin slices of fried bread; apples and pears if they were in season; and finally bread, and cheese with spiced cakes or wafers. If this is the kind of diet that Chaucer has in mind in the Franklin's household, then the famous metaphor seems appropriate: *It snewed in his hous of mete and drynke* (345).

A medieval feast from an illumination in the Luttrell Psalter, 1325–1340

The theme of epicurean indulgence is not confined to the Franklin. The Guildsmen have decided to take their own cook on the pilgrimage with them. Bearing in mind the spiritual purpose of the journey, what does this decision reveal of their most pressing concerns as they set out to the holy shrine? Their cook is given a brief description in his own right, which allows Chaucer another chance to show off his knowledge of culinary activities – how spices were used, the various means of cooking meat, and how to make a good hash or *blankmanger* – all of which presents yet another character whose skills are said to be among the best (in hyperbole): *For blankmanger, that made he with the beste* (387).

Love and devotion

The word *love* is repeated in a number of contexts, sometimes registering devotion to moral, religious and other noble causes, at other times with more than a hint of sexual desire and activity. Bearing in mind that devotion to God through holy pilgrimage should have been at the heart of the pilgrims' motivations, it is not surprising that the characters seem devoted to many different goals in their lives. Some of their attachments clearly undermine and make a mockery of religious loyalty; at other times there appears to be a celebration of the vitality and pleasure that can be associated with sexual love. Then there are other forms of devotion which reveal universal truths of human nature, such as the Doctor of Physic's love of gold and the Franklin's determination to *lyven in delit* (335).

Remind yourself first of all of the way in which the opening lines symbolically kindle the spirit of earthly and celestial love, as the young birds are woken and encouraged by the regenerating force of spring. (See Notes, pages 34–35.) Any suggestion that this will be a poem only about the awakening of spiritual love is modified by the lines that stress the pull of nature and earthly love.

Love is then identified very early in the portraits as a motivating force. The Knight, we are told, *loved chivalrie,/ Trouthe and honour, fredom and curteisie* (45–46).

We feel throughout his description that his love of God and his sense of the purpose of pilgrimage are correct and appropriate. Love, for him, is defined as service. Devotion is in evidence in equally strong measure in the portraits of the Clerk and the Ploughman. In the description of the Clerk, Chaucer writes: *Of studie took he moost cure and moost heede* (303), and of the Ploughman: *God loved he best with al his hoole herte* (533).

Although the word *love* is not used in the description of the Parson (477–528), the entire portrait reveals his unrelenting devotion to the laws of Christ.

But these four characters are exceptions. Look again at line 12: *Thanne longen folk to goon on pilgrimages*. If the Knight, the Clerk, the Parson and the Ploughman are the only four pilgrims who genuinely reveal religious devotion as the reason for their presence, then what are the motives of the others?

Activity

There are many ways in which love is presented. Discuss how love is presented in one particular way.

Discussion

As you approach the activity, give some thought to the varied meanings that the word *love* can have in human life. 'Devotion' has already been suggested, implying 'duty' and 'service'. How important are desire, motivation, obsession? Consider also relationships and how they are treated, particularly romance, courtship and marriage. You will also need to refer back to the section on the Church, recognizing the ways in which some of these pilgrims fell short of expectations of their service to God.

The following are some questions and references to consider.

- Are the Squire's youthful lustiness and courtly accomplishments (all designed to win him favour with women) natural in a young man, or do they come across as excessive and overpowering, to some extent undermining the sense of service so evident in his father?
- What can we learn about the traditions of courtly romance from

some of the lines that describe the Prioress (118–162)? (There is a full discussion of the Prioress on page 133, and detailed analysis of her apparent courtliness in the Notes on page 44.)

- The first lines in the poem to reveal corruption are 212–217, which would appear beyond doubt to suggest that the Friar, who would have vowed to remain celibate, has seduced young women and was *biloved and famulier... with worthy wommen of the toun*. How critical of the Friar do you think Chaucer is?
- You have already considered the motivating forces that inspired the so-called mercantile group of pilgrims, culminating in the explicit reference to love of gold at line 444.
- What might the Wife of Bath's motives be for her attendance on a pilgrimage, and why has she been on so many? What do we learn about marriage and sex from her portrait? What are Chaucer's motives for the inclusion of a strikingly colloquial innuendo when he assures us:

> Of remedies of love she knew per chaunce,
> For she koude of that art the olde daunce.   (475–476)

There is a fuller discussion of the Wife of Bath on page 135.
- The portrait of the Summoner is possibly the strongest caricature, designed perhaps to satirize the detestable practices of this cruel ecclesiastical role. Do you find it interesting that this portrait should include so many explicit references to sex? How different are they in tone from the sensual vitality and energy that comes across in the earlier account of the Squire?
- We have seen in the Notes (page 81) that there is no simple explanation of the sexuality of the Pardoner. The description is certainly not explicit (in spite of the apparent phallic pun in the phrase *stif burdoun*, 673) as to whether he and the Summoner are homosexual partners; nor is it clear that the way he is physically described – as being very effeminate – reveals his sexuality. Do you think there is enough evidence for the speculation that critics have entered into?

Characters and characterization

Any attempt to understand how characterization works in the poem is bound to differ from the study of most other literature for the simple reason that the bulk of the poem concentrates on descriptions of characters, through the portraits. A large part of the poem sets out explicitly just to present characters.

Derek Pearsall, in his chapter 'Some Portraits' (*The Canterbury Tales*, see Further Reading), reminds us that, by comparison with other medieval writers, Chaucer's 'ordering of details' in the portraits is unsystematic. In his view, 'comment on different aspects of physical appearance, behaviour, array, opinion, attitude, inward moral life and professional occupation is presented in the order in which it seems to have occurred to the memory of the observer'.

While there are some recurring and common features, such as descriptions of clothing, physical features and actions, the overall effect is informal, almost as if Chaucer were noticing features at random. But perhaps we should not confuse randomness with lack of purpose. On the contrary, he uses the haphazardry to good effect, by appearing to be slipping into the conversation (overall the descriptions do give the impression of being a conversation) comments of his own which can have a striking effect. In the description of the Wife of Bath, notice how he starts with the comment that *she was somdel deef, and that was scathe* (446), before describing her work as a cloth-maker, followed by her attitude to attendance at the altar in church. There is then some description of what she wears and he returns to brief comments about her physical appearance, again rather at random. At line 458 we are told that she has a red complexion, and at 468 that she is *Gat-tothed* – which in her own prologue she says is a sign of sexual desire. These unsystematic comments which pepper the descriptions give us fleeting glimpses of the nature of the characters and give the narrator the role of casual observer.

'Unsystematic' may be a way of describing the composition of the portraits, but critics have, on the other hand, pointed to the way in which many of them are built around a unifying point of focus; how many of them are 'enlarged' or exaggerated, suggesting a superiority to the characters which makes them less individual and more a type; and how the random comments from Chaucer are delivered with deliberate suddenness to gain dramatic or ironic impact.

Activity

How do the first two of these features, the unifying point of focus and the exaggerated traits, work?

Discussion

Try to identify the most notable examples of the unifying point of focus, for example the Knight's *worthynesse*; the Friar's *wantownesse*; the Reeve's bad temper; the Pardoner's hypocrisy. In what ways do all the elements of the description contribute to these main traits?

Virtually all of the characters are described by exaggerated superlatives. They are often the best or most noteworthy of their types or professions, a point of style which can characterize them more as types than individuals, although this is sometimes ironic. You could choose examples of this technique from nearly all the descriptions, but here are a few suggestions for you to analyse.

- The Friar:

    In alle the ordres foure is noon that kan
    So muchel of daliaunce and fair langage.   (210–211)

- The Sergeant of the Law:

    So greet a purchasour was nowher noon   (318)

- The Summoner:

    A bettre felawe sholde men noght fynde.   (648)

129

Is there a tone of irony in any of these lines?

What does the exaggeration achieve? Clearly, although the pilgrims may be drawn from a cross-section of society, they are by no means ordinary folk. However individual some of them may become through the realistic descriptions, many of them are presented as superior versions of their professions or 'types'. As has been shown, this tendency is completely idealized in, for example, the Knight, who becomes worthiness personified. Through this technique Chaucer either seems to celebrate many of the characters' human qualities or condemns them through the use of irony.

The use of sudden intervention, like lines 'out of the blue', is another striking technique. This has the effect not only of reasserting Chaucer's own role in the poem, but also of delivering a critical and sometimes dramatic comment on the individual pilgrim (see page 133). Often these unexpected thoughts interrupt other parts of the descriptions, as if Chaucer has suddenly been struck by a train of thought, perhaps sparked by something earlier in what he was saying, before returning to the main theme. Sometimes it is quite mild, as in the cases of the Monk, *Now certeinly he was a fair prelaat* (204), and the Friar, *Somwhat he lipsed, for his wantownesse* (264).

On other occasions there is an ironic or harsh quality to the tone, as if Chaucer is mocking the character, for example with the Merchant, *But, sooth to seyn, I noot how men hym calle* (284), and the Sergeant of the Law, *Of his array telle I no lenger tale* (330).

Activity

1   Analyse three portraits of different types of pilgrims – perhaps one of the ecclesiastical pilgrims, one mercantile and one of the women. Identify the similarities and variations in the techniques used to describe the pilgrims.

Show what the different techniques reveal about their characters.

2   How far are the characters presented as individuals and how much as types or representatives of their trade, calling or class?

Discussion

Many features of characterization will be familiar to you in literature, such as the connections between dress or clothing and character type, the role of complexion and physical appearance and sometimes the tone of voice or the way the characters speak.

Be aware that some of the portraits display a full range of what we might term 'individualizing techniques'. This is arguably the case among those whom Chaucer might have considered more significant, or at least more worthy of note: the Prioress, the Monk, the Friar, the Wife of Bath, the Reeve, the Summoner and the Pardoner. In each of these cases they are realized as highly individualized characters through their physical, behavioural and occupational features. At the opposite extreme there are completely idealized characters such as the Knight, the Parson and the Ploughman, who have very few individualizing or personal features. The Knight is a personification of chivalry. There is nothing in his description to individualize the Parson; nor anything personal about the Ploughman, the realism in his case rather earnestly concentrating on his labour: *That hadde ylad of dong ful many a fother* (530).

Others appear to be positioned somewhere between these two extremes. There are predictable traits that seem entirely in character, such as the Shipman's brutality and the Miller's brawn. Which characters appear to you to be the most individual?

There are other curious ways – perhaps they are even unique to the *General Prologue* – in which characterization happens through Chaucer's direct observations and descriptions. He frequently notices the way the pilgrims ride their horses, for example, or the position they take in the company en route, although even this sort of observation requires a certain amount of poetic licence as it is information he would have gleaned from the journey as a whole, rather than just the night in the Tabard, which this part of the poem concentrates on.

What does the Monk's horse tell us about its owner (207)? Notice the obvious association between the Clerk's horse and his need of a good meal at lines 287–288. Enjoy the description of the Shipman's awkwardness as he tries to come to terms with travel by land at line

390. How do we better picture the Wife of Bath's demeanour from the line *Upon an amblere esily she sat* (469)? In what way is the Ploughman made even more dependable by the description of his mare? Does the brief reference make him seem unassuming?

Even more characteristic is the flamboyant account of the Miller leading the pilgrimage, blowing his bagpipe, at lines 565–566. This contrasts directly with the Reeve (622), and it is hardly surprising that during the telling of the tales these two characters should come to blows.

You will also be aware of the ways in which the characters are brought to life through descriptions of their actions and their professional activities.

But characterization through the use of what we might now want to call 'pen portraits' is a more complex matter when you consider the amount of detail that Chaucer finds for the pilgrims. To get to grips with this point, reflect on the nature of the poem as both an observed and a fictional experience (although of course there is a twist because the observations are also fictional). There is simply too much detail about each of the characters – some of it from their pasts or about aspects of their behaviour which we cannot imagine being evident on the night in question at the Tabard. Critics have noticed that the layering of (apparent) detailed observation with wider fiction allows Chaucer to shift points of view as a character himself, one of the pilgrims. Unless we are to imagine that Chaucer has cross-examined each of the pilgrims before writing (or saying) anything about them, we accept that he has created fictional characters much like the writers, in later centuries, of novels.

The descriptions of the Friar and the Prioress illustrate the point. The bulk of the lines used on the Friar portray his corrupt form of life – almost a narrative in itself. Towards the end of the portrait his appearance and clothing are observed, but only after a long fictional account of what he does in life. While we might accept that Chaucer could have observed the Prioress's small dogs, we surely do not imagine that he has witnessed anyone painfully striking one of them with a stick. The Wife of Bath's headscarves and stockings would have been on show in the Tabard, but not her aggressive behaviour at the church altar, nor her history of pilgrimages.

The development of these fictions – sometimes termed 'illusions' – gives Chaucer ample opportunity to characterize himself as a pilgrim. This comes about noticeably through interjections, interruptions or lines of deviation, as if a sudden thought has occurred to him or as if he warms to a cause or point of view. See where you can find these personal interventions in the descriptions of the Monk, the Merchant, the Clerk, the Sergeant of the Law, the Cook, the Wife of Bath, and the Parson, some of which have already been identified. There are telling personal comments about both the Summoner:

> A bettre felawe sholde men noght fynde. (648)

> But wel I woot he lyed right in dede (659)

and the Pardoner:

> I trowe he were a geldyng or a mare. (691)

None of these comments from Chaucer the pilgrim would have been possible without the elaborately imagined personas he creates for each of the other pilgrims.

The two women

The only descriptions of female characters, of the Prioress and the Wife of Bath, are celebrated examples of irony and humour. The Prioress is a nun presented in a detailed style which critics have suggested is associated more with courtly elegance than religious devotion. The Wife of Bath is a formidable cloth-maker presented in a robust and flamboyant style that calls into question the motives for her pilgrimage.

The accounts appear to reveal the vanity and aspirations of the two women (although be aware that critics have not proved the case for ironic courtliness in the Prioress beyond all doubt). Both portraits touch upon another powerful theme of the poem: the motivating force of the need for esteem and recognition, a theme we also find in the portrait of the five Guildsmen.

The Prioress is described through her femininity, as if she

PRIORESS.

The illustration of the Prioress from the Ellesmere manuscript

were the heroine of a medieval romance in the disguise of an ecclesiastical calling. Her studied singing, the style of French she speaks, her meticulous table manners, her sympathetic treatment of small animals and her elegantly adorned mode of dress all suggest a benign person but one who has been practising the modesty and quiet demeanour of the heroines of courtly romance. Madame Eglentyne's name itself – hers by choice – is more likely to have originated from a character in a romance than from one modelled on religious life. The stock phrase *symple and coy* (119) denotes the kind of quiet but possibly seductive modesty of the courtly romance heroine. There are numerous details of her physical appearance such as her shapely nose (*tretys*, 152), sparkling eyes (*greye as glas*, 152), small, soft, round mouth and her fair forehead, which, however broad it was, should not even have been uncovered.

Part of the irony arises because the traits in her character do suggest virtuous behaviour such as modesty, charity, pity and generosity, but hardly that this devotion is motivated by her duty to God. Why would a courtly heroine behave in such a pleasant and attractive manner?

Courtly love as a tradition meant that love was almost a specialized art. The male lover would be humble, obedient to his intended lady's slightest wish. He would often have to tolerate rejection of his advances and sometimes women would delight in making themselves unattainable. This was supposed to mean that, if their affection could finally be won, they would be prized more highly. Thus, love was rather like the feudal society; just as dependents on the land had to do service to their lord, so the lover was a kind of slave to his lady. Because of this, the art of 'wooing' was a polite, courteous and reverential type of behaviour. Women would be coy and even artful. Above all, their behaviour would have been highly self-conscious.

The Wife of Bath is less modest about establishing herself in her community. In the parish of St Michael-juxta-Bathon, the cloth industry flourished, and here, as elsewhere in medieval England, women were active in its pursuit. As well as being one of these prominent women in the parish, she is also assertive and dominant. If the Prioress is motivated to behave quietly and modestly in a courtly manner as a way of satisfying her vanity, the Wife of Bath shows no similar restraint. There is a lack of shame in all that she does: she insists on being the first at the altar; she wears ostentatious clothing; and she is willing to be outrageously frank about her past.

Study the characteristics of the Wife of Bath. In the first instance, if she is deaf, would this tend to draw attention to her or allow her to merge into the background? In her skills at weaving, she is described as superior to those in the major European cloth-making centres of Ypres and Ghent. We may want to speculate on who made this claim. Given her determination and competitiveness at the offertory, how do we imagine she would behave if she were ever denied this superior status in her profession? What does her Sunday clothing reveal

WIFE OF BATH.

The illustration of the Wife of Bath from the Ellesmere manuscript

about her personality, and why do you think Chaucer decides to give an estimate of the weight of her *coverchiefs* (453–455)? Do we grasp what her mood would have been like if ever she were not afforded high status in her life and work?

> certeyn so wrooth was she
> That she was out of alle charitee.   **(451–452)**

She has had considerable and varied sexual experience: five husbands, even without mentioning *oother compaignye in youthe* (461); there are hints of lechery on her previous pilgrimages; and she has profound knowledge of cures for love-sickness and a well-tuned understanding of the ways of love and sex (*For she koude of that art the olde daunce*, 476). Alongside the Squire, therefore, she links most directly with the interest aroused in a sensual response to life in the opening lines of the poem. For a woman so proud, flamboyant and overbearing, how well prepared do you think she is for pilgrimage? Is there evidence that her ambitions are pointing in other directions as she sets off to the tomb of the *hooly blisful martir* (17)?

Activity

Do you agree that vanity is a characteristic of the Prioress and the Wife of Bath? What evidence is there of vanity in other characters? Choose one other example.

Discussion

Like the Wife of Bath, many of the male characters seek to promote their own causes or further their own interests as a result of self-satisfaction or through the need for power or control. This is a trait to be found in the Merchant, the Sergeant of the Law and the Guildsmen. The Manciple and the Reeve are also characters who like to exert influence. Yet traits of self-consciousness and individual affectation are never as strong as in the detailed and intricate portraits of the Prioress and the Wife of Bath.

Both descriptions, with different points of emphasis, reveal attitudes towards women in the Middle Ages. The Prioress, who would initially have been elected to be the head of her convent, with the approval of the bishop, would have been partly presiding over an order that had received an endowment and partly overseeing this order as a working institution in the community. Just like a well-to-do woman in the town or countryside, her job would have been to supervise the property of the convent – its farms, stables and fields – not unlike the role of the Reeve, in fact. Many prioresses were highly respected in their areas, enjoying the same privileges as lords of manors.

Although many prioresses were never distracted from the strictness of their vows, which required contemplative isolation from the fashions and influences of the secular world, others, because of their contact with the outside world, became very worldly – a characteristic explored also in the Monk and the Friar. If the Monk's worldliness is a highly masculine response to life, with his hunting, gaming, sporting and drinking, the Prioress's is intensely and coquettishly feminine. Her secular approach is based on an impression she has of herself taking part in the peace-time activities of courtly love. Her intricate, detailed and self-conscious behaviour is a fastidious imitation of the sort of noblewoman who, in many a great medieval household, would have occupied herself with enriching the cultural and literary lives of the nobility, drawing attention to herself as a potential lover for male suitors diverted from military service. Such men, with time and leisure on their hands, would have been intent on proving their prowess in the struggles of love and courtship.

None of this is to suggest that she is revealed as a sexual character. The emphasis is on imitation of courtliness, which would have been wholly out of keeping with her religious calling. Is it therefore vanity which motivates her to behave with such affectation?

If the vain mannerisms of the Prioress cause us to smile, with the Wife of Bath there is overt sexuality. There are oblique references to sex elsewhere among the descriptions of the pilgrims: the young Squire who sleeps *namoore than dooth a nyghtyngale* (98); the Friar who *hadde maad ful many a mariage/ Of yonge wommen at his owene cost* (212–213); the Miller who tells lewd stories (560–561); and the Summoner – *As hoot he was and lecherous as a sparwe* (626). But nowhere is sexual desire and drive so evident as in the description of the past – and probably the present intentions! – of the Wife of Bath. A traditional view of female sexuality was that, once tempted, a woman's true sexual nature would be revealed. In Boccaccio's *Decameron*, also of the late fourteenth century (1348–1353), there are numerous innocent sexual heroines. Once their virginity is relinquished, they become insatiable, frequently reducing men to a state of impotence. The *Decameron* is an earlier Italian work, also a collection of tales, which Chaucer may have had access to while in Italy.

The Wife of Bath expresses more about her controlling, but uncontrolled, sexual urge in her own tale and its celebrated prologue. She is a woman of vigorous and exhausting sexual energy. As so often happens in Chaucer's way of characterization, we learn much about her main characteristic through traits of her behaviour in other parts of her life. What do you imagine of her treatment of husbands and lovers from some of the other things we learn about her, for example the way she dominates in her profession, the way she brushes the whole parish aside at the altar? What do the excesses in her clothing and her record of attendance on pilgrimages suggest about her?

Style

One reason why a variety of styles is needed is because of Chaucer's window on such a range of characters drawn from so many walks of life and from different social classes. How does his language deal with this variety of people, ranging from the chivalry of the Knight and courtliness of the Prioress at one end of the social scale to the ditch-digging of the Ploughman and lewd buffoonery of the Miller at the other?

There are some features of style that stand out, some of which have already been mentioned in the discussion of characterization. Look for the use of hyperbole or exaggeration: so many of the pilgrims are the best, unsurpassed or incomparable in what they do. This kind of language does seem to suggest Chaucer's delight in the power of human achievement.

Hyperbole also has the effect of identifying the characters as types, highlighting common characteristics of their role, profession or calling, rather than of them as individuals.

Consider how these characteristics provide an impression of three professions. We learn that there is no better purchaser of land than the Sergeant of the Law (318). The portrait of the Franklin is completed with the line that defines his high social standing: *Was nowher swich a worthy vavasour* (360). The Cook's portrait also finishes with a hyperbole: *For blankmanger, that made he with the beste* (387).

Similar to hyperbole, there is a delightful tendency in the style to strengthen impressions of the pilgrims with intensifiers that qualify and quantify their attributes and achievements. Consider how this technique provides such a vivid impression of the Squire:

> So hoote he lovede that by nyghtertale
> He sleep namoore than dooth a nyghtyngale. (97–98)

The Clerk's virtuous commitment to his studies is equally strongly characterized:

> **Of studie took he moost cure and moost heede.**
> **Noght o word spak he moore than was neede** (303–304)

As is the case later in many of the tales, there is considerable use of realism; the language of farmyard and kitchen is used as effectively as that of court or crusade. This realistic approach has been termed 'familiarity' or 'provincialism'. At times it is highly colloquial, at times proverbial, and commonly expressed in imagery; consider the image Chaucer uses to stress the exemplary approach to life shown by the Parson to his flock (500).

Where imagery is used, there is both metaphor and simile, but Chaucer does at times appear more at ease with simile as a literary device, almost as if his images need to be drawn out in natural conversation. See the Monk: *men myghte his brydel heere/ Gynglen... as dooth the chapel belle* (169–171), and the Clerk: *As leene was his hors as is a rake* (287). Use of simile fits too with the conversational style, which is also evident through personal intervention from the narrator.

Can you at times detect another kind of realism when, for example, the tone and intonation of a pilgrim's voice is suggested? There are also cases when the punctuation, the enjambement and onomatopoeia give an impression of the character's actions. We might have a vivid sense that the Wife of Bath's complexion suggests a breathless hustle and busyness; that the lines used to describe the Parson suggest his tireless trudge into all corners of his parish; that we can visualize the Ploughman at his willing toil – *He wolde thresshe, and therto dyke and delve* (536) – and the stoutly built Miller breaking down the door *at a rennyng* (551).

Linked to realism is a feature of the style sometimes termed 'encyclopaedism'. Earlier we looked at Chaucer's impressive display of his wide knowledge of the world. This outpouring of detail has the effect of lending a deliberate doctrinal air to his work (as if he were setting out to teach, lecture or even preach). It is a stylistic technique used frequently in the tales in order to provide 'exemplars' – catalogues of argument to strengthen the authority of the speaker. A similar device is the use of 'inventory'. This involves a list of characteristics, such as personal features, complexion, physique, dress, apparel, tools of a trade, all of which offer not just a physical impression of the pilgrims but indicate character as well, and of course contribute to an impression of the type as well as the individual. The most celebrated example of this can be seen in the description of the Knight from line 51. This is by far the longest; shorter, but no less effective, examples can be found in the description of the Squire's courtliness (95–96) and the Reeve's farm management (595–598).

The tendency to take stock of a character originated in the high style of French romances which Chaucer consciously used as a model for his art.

Irony

The unifying mixture of styles – the calm juxtaposition of conventional high literary style with the realism of everyday life – allows Chaucer the constant possibility of ironic comment on the pilgrims. Their pedestals can quickly be removed, their self-importance reduced, and when necessary, their immorality or greed crushingly exposed. In addition to the mockery of types of character as in estates satire, Chaucer displays a sharply perceptive awareness of human nature.

Is the main subject of the poem – pilgrimage – treated ironically? The nature of the pilgrimage calls into question the assertion that very many of these pilgrims would be in the saddle *with ful devout corage* (22). Many of them, we assume, will be failing in their hearts and minds to aspire to a holy state of readiness for their task ahead. We suspect that for some the journey will be a diversion rather than a contemplation.

Activity

Identify three different ways in which Chaucer is being ironic. These could be about individual pilgrims, about general themes or about the tone of the irony.

What sort of impression does the irony give about the start of a holy journey?

Discussion

An enduring interpretation of the characters is that of self-interest. As you have seen there are honourable exceptions, but as they ride *Unto the Wateryng of Seint Thomas* (826), we are left with an impression of many characters unlikely to spend their time in contemplative reflection, an impression enhanced in any event by the Host's proposal as to how they should pass their time.

Yet this is not to suggest that Chaucer sets out to judge harshly all the characters nor condemn all their behaviour. His ambivalent attitude to the self-denial of the Clerk and his enthusiasm for the vigour of the Monk remind us that Chaucer's own outlook on life was far from austere. His irony and mockery are at times mild, suggesting merely that the motivations of human beings are complex and their personalities full of contradictions, many of which are comic. But even though he may poke fun at them, he frequently warms to their creativity: just as the sap rises at the start of the poem, so many of his characters reward the world with their contributions. Some of their activities may be morally questionable – some much more than others – but their energy is never in doubt.

How strong is Chaucer's mockery? As has been suggested, it may be that he can poke fun at his characters without having to criticize them directly. Some characters fool themselves. You may want to consider the portraits of the Prioress, the Merchant and the Guildsmen in this respect.

Sometimes Chaucer points to a physical feature which, he might well claim, has merely involved observation (*so as it semed me*, 39). But often we sense another purpose. This can be the revelation of a character trait somehow symbolized in a feature of appearance, such as the Prioress's brooch (160), the Miller's nostrils (557), or the emasculated bodily features of the Pardoner (688–690).

What do you think of the way that the most roguish characters are described in the most admiring language? Why did the Friar hear confession so sweetly (221), the Merchant speak with such ceremony (274), and why was the Shipman *certeinly... a good felawe* (395)?

Do references to love maintain a central irony in the poem? The love of God should have been uppermost in the minds of the pilgrims, and certainly there are some noble examples of love, for example the Knight, the Parson and the Clerk. But do some of the other references mock the notion that religious love is at the heart of this event? Just as the opening lines do, the style at times juxtaposes spiritual and earthly concerns in the descriptions. For instance, the Monk loves to hunt:

> And whan he rood, men myghte his brydel heere
> Gynglen in a whistlynge wynd als cleere
> And eek as loude as dooth the chapel belle. (169–171)

As readers we are faced with a choice of perspectives here, reminding us that Chaucer's irony is often mild. Is the Monk's love of earthly sport inappropriate, admirable or even potentially redemptive, if by the example of his hunting he calls other men to God? Chaucer leaves his readers to draw their own conclusions, although of course there are portraits where the tone of irony becomes more mocking and damning.

Critical views

Critics and commentators have examined the *General Prologue* from a variety of viewpoints to try to explain what Chaucer might have intended by the poem. Here are some of the approaches they have taken.

Estates satire – a possible source and model

Among the various interpretations of the poem and the explanations of its derivation, the model of estates satire has come to be seen as more important. There was an assumption that the *General Prologue* was an original idea, but Jill Mann, in particular, has questioned this in her book *Chaucer and Medieval Estates Satire* (see Further Reading). 'Estate' here means something along the lines of 'station', 'class' or 'status'. In medieval life people were expected to be content with their own status and their behaviour needed to be kept in line with what was appropriate to it. This expectation was believed to have been divinely ordained (decreed by God), and the good of society was dependent on everybody observing the rules of their status. On page 1 of her book, Jill Mann comments:

> I shall be claiming that the *Prologue* is an example of a neglected Medieval genre – that both its form and its content proclaim it to be part of the literature dealing with the 'estates' of society.

An important point to bear in mind is that, however vivid some of the characters become, they are all identified only by their profession or role in life, for example: *A Sergeant of the Lawe…/ Ther was also* (309–311); *A Frankeleyn was in his compaignye* (331).

Jill Mann not only thought that Chaucer used the model of portraits to criticize society – through the faults associated with each 'estate' – but also that he may have drawn some of his materials from earlier rhetorical writings where people were described through their profession or estate.

Thus, even though there are many original lines and ideas in the poem, its origins may not have been at all new. (See page 91, and Notes, page 33).

Understanding of the universal nature of human life

Whereas the origins in estates satire provide a more precise explanation of what Chaucer was attempting to achieve, appreciations in earlier centuries often focused on the way in which the poem was able to present universal characteristics of human nature. This is a view that emphasizes the fact that certain types of human behaviour will always be evident in any age. The pilgrims become *personifications*, revealing traits of human nature which show the full extent of human life. The language expresses these traits, either directly, indirectly or humorously, through the irony or satire. In this respect, notice how the Knight is an enduring hero. William Blake, the great eighteenth- and early nineteenth-century English poet, said of the Knight:

> **He has spent his life in the field; he has ever been a conqueror, and is that species of character which in every age stands as the guardian of man against the oppressor.**
> *A Descriptive Catalogue of Pictures, Poetical and*
> *Historical Inventions,* **1809**

In the same way that every society has had, has now and will always have its heroes and guardians, so it will always have characters like the Miller who will use 'brutal strength and courage' to exert their power over others in order to become rich and strong.

With some of the portraits, the revealing of human nature becomes more complex. Some of the more detailed and individualized descriptions show a lot more about inner motives and personalities, possibly establishing Chaucer as the first in a long line of English writers capable of exposing human frailty. The Monk, the Friar and the Prioress are often cited as three such characters whose complex natures are revealed.

The unity of the poem

By its nature, the central purpose of the *General Prologue* is difficult to define. Critics have made great efforts to discover its unity. Consider the problem. The poem covers:

- a romantic and idealized opening passage about the regeneration of spring
- a long section of descriptive portraits representing a cross-section of medieval professions
- the start of a story about pilgrimage
- a conversation in an inn leading to a storytelling challenge.

Another factor frequently considered in the efforts to define the central purpose is the role of Chaucer himself (see page 101).

A great deal has been written, with much speculation, about

the opening passage, in particular how the sensuous theme of regeneration, which is clearly not set in the real world, transfers to the here and now, and what the links are with the pious purpose of pilgrimage. The analyses and explanations have suggested that:

- there are contrasts between the vigour and physical vitality encapsulated by the opening, and sickness (*seeke*, 18) – ultimately the purpose of pilgrimage, which interferes with or blemishes this ideal and uplifting landscape
- above all, the portraits expose human ambiguity, suggesting that human beings reveal a yawning gap between positive and negative influences, or between noble and misguided motives; the gap is sometimes evident within the nature of the characters themselves (the Monk, the Friar) and sometimes laid bare in the contrasts between the characters (the Parson, the Pardoner)
- the portraits are directly a parody of the piety (spiritual correctness and faith) needed for pilgrimage, as is the diverting challenge at the end.

Many critics have also celebrated and delighted in the power of human impulse. However impure the pilgrims' motives may have been, however unready for pilgrimage, so many of them show that human life is full of freshness, energy, purpose and determination, similar to and maybe even linked with the sap that rises as described in the first few lines.

Always bear in mind that the *General Prologue* is not a complete work; ultimately any sense of its unity has to be considered alongside the whole of *The Canterbury Tales*.

Controversies about individual portraits

Some of the portraits are easier to interpret than others. The more complex ones – of four characters in particular – have given rise to considerable research and speculation, especially on the nature of irony.

It is important to recognize that there are no single explanations to some of these controversies. Although we may make assertions about the effects of Chaucer's portraits, these have to be based on speculative evidence and for each argument in favour of one interpretation, there are as many alternatives.

These controversies have focused on:

- whether the Knight is a noble hero or a mercenary (see Notes, page 39)
- whether the purpose behind the portrait of the Prioress is satirical or simply one full of admiration (see Notes, pages 44–45)
- the sexual inclinations of the Summoner and the Pardoner (see Notes, page 81).

A Note on Chaucer's English

Chaucer's English has so many similarities with Modern English that it is unnecessary to learn extensive tables of grammar. With a little practice, and using the glosses provided, it should not be too difficult to read the text. Nevertheless, it would be foolish to pretend that there are no differences. The remarks which follow offer some information, hints and principles to assist students who are reading Chaucer's writings for the first time, and to illustrate some of the differences (and some of the similarities) between Middle and Modern English. More comprehensive and systematic treatments of this topic are available in *The Riverside Chaucer* and in D. Burnley, *A Guide to Chaucer's Language*.

1 Inflections

These are changes or additions to words, usually endings, which provide information about number (whether a verb or a noun is singular or plural) tense or gender.

a) Verbs

In the **present** tense most verbs add −e in the first person singular (e.g. *I ryde*), −est in the second person singular (e.g. *thou sayest*), −eth in the third person singular (*she sayeth*) and −en in the plural. This can be summarized as follows:

	Middle English	Modern English
Singular	1 I telle 2 Thou tellest 3 He/She/It telleth	I tell You tell He/She/It tells
Plural	1 We tellen 2 Ye tellen 3 They tellen	We tell You tell They tell

As you can see, Middle English retains more inflections than Modern English, but the system is simple enough. Old English, the phase of the language between around 449 AD, when the Angles first came to Britain, and about 1100, had many more inflections.

In describing the **past** tense it is necessary to begin by making a distinction, which still applies in Modern English, between strong and weak verbs. **Strong verbs** form their past tense by changing their stem (e.g. I sing, I sang; You drink, you drank; he fights, he fought; we throw, we threw), while **weak verbs** add to the stem (I want, I wanted; you laugh, you laughed; he dives, he dived).

In the past tense in Middle English, strong verbs change their stems (e.g. *sing* becomes *sang* or *song*) and add –e in the second person singular (e.g. *thou songe*) and –en in the plural (e.g. *they songen*). Weak verbs add –de or –te (e.g. *fele* becomes *felte*, *here* becomes *herde*) with –st in the second person singular (e.g. *thou herdest*) and –n in the plural (e.g. *they felten*). The table below compares the past tense in Middle and Modern English for strong and weak verbs.

Strong verbs		
	Middle English Present stem: 'sing'	**Modern English**
Singular	1 I sange (or soonge) 2 Thou songe 3 He/She/It sange	I sang (or sung) You sang He/She/It sang
Plural	1 We songen 2 Ye songen 3 They songen	We sang You sang They sang

−Weak verbs		
	Middle English Present stem: 'here'	**Modern English** hear
Singular	1 I herde 2 Thou herdest 3 He/She/It herde	I heard You heard He/She/It heard
Plural	1 We herden 2 Ye herden 3 They herden	We heard You heard They heard

The past tense can also be formed using the auxiliary verb *Gan* plus the past participle (e.g. *gan... preye* [301]: prayed). In a very few cases *Gan* means 'began' but in most cases it indicates a past tense. Some verbs add initial *y* to their past participle (e.g. *yronne* [8], *yfalle* [25]).

b) Nouns and adjectives

Nouns mostly add −s or −es for plural (e.g. *songes* [95]) and possessive (e.g. *lordes* [47]). There are no apostrophes in Middle English! Some nouns add −en for plural (e.g. *eyen* [152]). Although (unlike modern French or German) nouns do not take grammatical gender in Middle English, some nouns do add −e for feminine (e.g. *tappestere* [241], barmaid).

Some adjectives add −e in the plural (e.g. *fresshe* [90]).

c) Personal pronouns

The forms of the personal pronouns are somewhat different from those used in Modern English and are worth recording in full:

		Subject	Object	Possessive
Singular	1	I, ich	me	myn, my
	2	Thou, thow	thee	thyn, thy
	3 masculine	He	hym, him	his
	3 feminine	She	her	hir, hire
	3 neuter	It, hit	it, hit	his
Plural	1	We	us	owre, our, owres
	2	Ye	you, yow	your, youres
	3	They	hem	hire, here

Remember that the distinction between *thou* and *you* in Middle English often involves politeness and social relationship as well as number. This is similar to modern French or German. Thus *thou* forms are used with friends, family and social inferiors, *you* forms with strangers or superiors.

2 Relative pronouns

The main **relative pronouns** found are *that* and *which*. In translating *that* it is often wise to try out a range of Modern English equivalents, such as *who, whom, which*. The prefix *ther*– in such words as *therto* and *therwith* often refers back to the subject matter of the previous phrase. *Therto* may be translated as 'in addition to all that' or 'in order to achieve that'.

3 Impersonal construction

With certain verbs the **impersonal construction** is quite common (e.g. *Me thynketh* [37], it seems to me; *hym leste*, it pleased him [787]).

4 Reflexive pronouns

Many verbs can be used with a **reflexive pronoun**, a pronoun which refers back to the subject (as in modern French or German) and which may, depending on the verb employed, be translated or understood as part of the verb (e.g. *born hym weel* [87], conducted himself well; *peyned hire* [139], took pains).

5 Extra negatives

In Middle English extra **negatives** often make the negative stronger, whereas in Modern English double negatives cancel each other out (e.g. *That no drope ne fille* [131], so that no drop fell).

6 Contraction

Sometimes negatives and pronouns merge with their associated verbs (e.g. *nas* from *ne was*, was not; *artow* from *art thou*, are you).

7 Word order

Middle English **word order** is often freer than Modern English, and in particular there is more inversion of subject and verb (e.g. *A Knyght ther was* [43], *Ful worthy was he* [47]). In analysing difficult sentences you should first locate the verb (A in the examples below), then its subject (B), then the object or complement (C). (Roughly, a verb which involves activity takes an object – he hit the ball, she gave him the book – while a verb which describes a state of affairs takes a complement – it was yellow, you look better.) Then you should put these elements together (D). It should be easier to see how the various qualifiers fit in (E).

In the sentence beginning at line 83, the verb (A) is *was*, the subject (B) *he*, the complement (C) *of evene lengthe*. Put together (D) this gives: he was moderately long. When we add the qualifier

(E) *Of his stature*, this changes to: he was moderately tall. We can then see that *wonderly delyvere* (wonderfully active, or agile) and *of greet strengthe* are further complements dependent on *he was*: he was moderately tall, wonderfully active and very strong. In most cases you will not need to analyse (or construe) a sentence like this, but if you are unsure this procedure may help you. A slightly harder example, which you might like to try, would be the sentence beginning at line 35.

The main verb (A) here is the impersonal *Me thynketh*; the subject (B) is *it*: it seems to me. The complement (C) is *acordaunt to resoun*, reasonable. The resulting construction (It seems to me reasonable...) requires another clause to complete the complement, in this case *To telle yow al the condicioun*. Once we have the main structure (D) (It seems to me reasonable to tell you the state) we can fit in the words and phrases which qualify and develop the point: (E) But nevertheless, while I have time, before I go any further into my story, **it seems to me reasonable to tell you the state** of all of them, as it appeared to me, who they were, their status, and the clothes they wore; and I shall begin with the knight.

The sentence beginning at line 19 is a much harder example.

A and B The main verb is the first word *Bifil* (it happened). This impersonal verb implies its own subject (it).

C *Bifil* must be linked to its complement (that a company came into the inn, [23–24]).

D From there we can derive the main structure: 'When I was in Southwark, it happened that a company, who intended to go to Canterbury, came into the inn'.

E Then we can find places for the various explanatory phrases: 'One day at that time of year when **I was in Southwark** at the Tabard inn, in a very pious spirit and ready to go on my pilgrimage to Canterbury, **it happened that a company** of twenty-nine, different sorts of people, but all pilgrims, **who** had been drawn into association by chance and **intended to ride to Canterbury, came into that inn** at night.'

8 Connection of clauses

Middle English often does not indicate **connection of clauses** as clearly as Modern English. In seeking to understand or in translating you may need to provide connecting words. (In the last three lines of the example above, for instance, I had to add the conjunctions *but* and *and*, and the relative pronoun *who*). On occasion you may have to provide verbs which have been omitted (particularly the verb 'to be' or verbs of motion) or regularize number or tense (in some Middle English sentences a subject can shift from singular to plural or a verb from present to past). For example, in line 50 (*And evere honoured for his worthynesse*) *he was* has to be understood as part of the sentence; in lines 856–8:

> And with that word we ryden forth oure weye,
> And he bigan with right a myrie cheere
> His tale anon, and seyde as ye may heere.

Chaucer can mix the past tense with the historic present (sometimes in telling a story we use the present tense, even though we and our audience know that the events occurred in the past) but a Modern English writer would have to maintain consistency at least within the sentence and usually within the paragraph as well. Chaucer's usage here (and with the implied words and the lack of connectives) may well be closer to spoken English than modern formal writing could be.

9 Change of meaning

Although most of the words which Chaucer uses are still current (often with different spellings) in Modern English, some of them have changed their meaning. In lines 1–4, for example, every word (except perhaps *engendred*: produced) corresponds to a Modern English word (*soote* = sweet), but the usual modern meanings of 'virtue' and 'liquor' would not be appropriate here. So it is a good idea to check the Notes or the Glossary even for words which look familiar. If you are interested in investigating the ways in which words change their meanings over time you can look at the quotations provided in large historical dictionaries, such as the *Oxford English Dictionary* or the *Shorter Oxford Dictionary* or in R.W. Burchfield, *The English Language* (Oxford, 1985), pp. 113–23, or G. Hughes, *Words in Time: A Social History of English Vocabulary* (Blackwell). Here are a few more examples from the *General Prologue*:

Middle English	(line number)	Meaning	Equivalent modern word
array	(41)	clothing, dress	array
aventure	(844)	chance	adventure
baillif	(603)	farm manager	bailiff
barge	(410)	ship, sea-going merchant vessel	barge
burdoun	(673)	bass accompaniment	burden
bynne	(593)	grain bin	bin[1]
carpe	(474)	talk	carp[2]
catel	(373)	property	cattle
clennesse	(506)	purity	cleanness
clerk	(285)	educated person, scholar	clerk
complexioun	(333)	temperament	complexion
cordial	(443)	medicine for the heart	cordial
countrefete	(139)	imitate	counterfeit
coy	(119)	quiet	coy
croppes	(7)	shoots (of plants)	crops
curious	(196, 577)	skilful, skilfully made	curious

1   In Modern English 'bin' on its own means 'rubbish bin'.
2   'Carp' is quite a rare word in Modern English, but it means 'complain', as in 'stop carping', where the Middle English word denotes speaking generally.

A Note on Pronunciation

The *General Prologue*, like other poems, benefits from being read aloud. Even if you read it aloud in a Modern English pronunciation you will get more from it, but Middle English was pronounced differently (the sounds of a language change over time at least as much as the vocabulary or the constructions) and it helps to make some attempt at a Middle English accent. The best way to learn this is to imitate one of the recordings (the tapes issued by Pavilion and Argo are especially recommended for this purpose). A few principles are given below; more can be found in *The Riverside Chaucer*.

1   In most cases you should pronounce all consonants (for example you should sound the 'k' in knight and the 'l' in half). But in words of French origin initial 'h' (as in *hostelrye*, [23], for example) should not be sounded, nor should 'g' in the combination 'gn' (as in *digne*, [141]). The combination 'gh', (as in *draughte* [135]), is best sounded 'ch' as in Modern English 'loch'.

2   In most cases all vowels are sounded, though a final 'e' may be silent because of elision with a vowel following (e.g. do not sound the second 'e' in *veyne in*, [3]) or because of the stress pattern of the line (e.g. in line 13, I would make the second 'e' in *palmeres* silent, but sound the final 'e' in *straunge*).

3   Two points of spelling affect pronunciation. When 'y' appears as a vowel, you should sound it as 'i' (see table on page 158). Sometimes a 'u' sound before 'n' or 'm' was written 'o' (because 'u' and 'n' looked very similar in the handwriting of the time). This means that *song* and *yong* should be pronounced 'sung' and 'yung'. This also applies in *comen* and *sonne* (as in their Modern English equivalents 'come' and 'son').

4 You will not go too far wrong with combinations of vowels, such as *ai*, *eu*, and *oy* if you sound them as in Modern English. There are significant exceptions (for example *hous* [252] and *mous* [144] should be pronounced with an *oo* sound) but it is not possible to establish reliable rules purely on the basis of the spelling.

5 The principal vowel sounds differ somewhat from Modern English. They are set out in the table below (adapted from Norman Davis's table in *The Riverside Shakespeare*). The table distinguishes long and short versions of each vowel. This distinction still applies in Modern English (consider the 'a' sounds in hat and father) but unfortunately it is often only possible to decide whether a particular vowel is long or short by knowing about the derivation of the word. Do not despair. Even a rough approximation will help you. Only experts in Middle English and related medieval languages have reliable Middle English accents, and even they cannot be sure that Chaucer would approve them.

Vowel	Middle English example	Modern equivalent sound
Long 'a'	stables(28) caas(323)	'a' in father
Short 'a'	Ram(8) nature(11)	'a' in hat
Long 'e'	he(45) been(64)	'a' in fate
Open 'e'	teche(308) heeth(606)	'e' in there
Short 'e'	tendre(7) wende(16)	'e' in set
Unstressed 'e'	sonne(7) londes(14)	'a' in about, 'e' in forgotten
Long 'i'	I(20) ryde(27)	'i' in machine
Short 'i'	licour(3) knyght(42)	'i' in sit
Long 'o'	fro(44) goode(74)	'o' in note
Open 'o'	hooly(17) goon(12)	'oa' in broad
Short 'o'	wol(42) croppes(7)	'o' in hot
Long 'u'	flour(4) foweles(9)	'oo' in boot
Short 'u'	ful(22) Juste(96)	'u' in put

Essay Questions

Worked questions

The two questions below are followed by some points you might address in your response.

Remember that whenever you are asked in essay questions to refer to a variety or number of pilgrims, it is best to discuss at least three in detail.

1 Examine the methods that Chaucer uses to influence our view of a variety of pilgrims.

Here are some ideas you might explore in your response:

- It is probably a good idea to focus on three types of portraits: first those in which he idealizes the pilgrims; second those where he is mildly ironic; and third where the tone becomes harshly satirical.
- It might also be worth considering a range of attitudes: say one portrait in which he makes the pilgrim stand out as a paragon of virtue; one which is complex, i.e. where there is plenty to condemn but where we sense admiration; and finally, one whom he condemns outright.
- On a broader basis, consider aspects of the conversational style Chaucer uses to mock or diminish the self-importance of some of the characters, even though you may decide not to explore these portraits in detail.
- This sort of general planning will help give an overall shape to your essay – one of the problems in writing essays on the *General Prologue* is that so much can be said rather randomly because that is the nature of the poem, so it is especially important to be clear what your examples are, otherwise essays can skim the surface.
- For the idealized characters, the Knight would be a good example. Deal with the concentration on his chivalry through

some of the typical techniques used in the portraits, such as his background and appearance. Be sure to show how this noble description presents an example of chivalric behaviour which leads us to admire him. You may of course wish to acknowledge the debate over the irony in the description.

- To consider a mildly ironic portrait, possibilities are the Prioress, the Monk, the Friar and the Merchant. Deal with the way in which specific lines establish the contrasts between how they should behave and how they actually behave. Make sure you are not too general: use very precise examples, such as the Prioress's table manners or the Monk's love of hunting. The irony is often achieved in the detail of the portrait rather than in any direct comment.

- In a similar way choose either the Summoner or the Pardoner for analysis of a pilgrim Chaucer appears to condemn.

- Try to argue why some characters are treated with mild irony even though they may have faults or shortcomings, whereas the Summoner or the Pardoner are dealt with more severely.

- Finally, refer to a small range of other characters such as the Clerk, the Miller or the Reeve, giving brief examples of how Chaucer's voice, aspects of their appearance and imagery contribute to the communication of his attitudes.

2 How does Chaucer establish a realistic impression of medieval England?

This question invites rather more in your response than simply listing the moments of realism. It is important to acknowledge the role of realism and to discuss the extent to which an impression of medieval life is a central purpose or a by-product of the overall intention of the poem.

- Start with the second part of the opening: establish how the poem is located in the Tabard; perhaps even contrast this with the more cosmic opening. You may also wish to consider the scene in the Tabard at the end of the poem.

- Discuss the context of the presentation of the portraits. In other words, avoid simply giving the impression that the poem is just a collection of portraits as if to represent the reality of medieval England.
- However, you will need to show that one of the great charms of the poem is that it does provide us, almost like an encyclopaedia, with evidence of how people lived. Choose three portraits to consider in detail, but make sure that they represent different areas of the medieval world, such as the land, the Church and the more urban or mercantile side of life.
- In these analyses of the techniques, consider: how the characters worked; the historical details outlining aspects of their professions; revelations about what they ate, drank, how they travelled and how they spent their time in the locations of their professions or callings; what they wore; how they spent their leisure time.
- You may like to reflect in your answer key themes such as money and class or status.
- Comment on the style and form of the poem, referring to Chaucer's conversational tone, showing how this contributes to the realism, the imagery and to the many lists displaying his knowledge of a particular aspect of life.

Sample questions

The following questions are for you to try.

1 From the portraits of the ecclesiastical pilgrims, to what extent do you find that the Church is shown to be corrupt?

2 Consider closely any two pilgrims whose behaviour appears to contradict their calling in life.

3 Is it the case that Chaucer can both mock and admire his characters?

4 How effectively does Chaucer establish characters who are rogues?

5 The pilgrims have variously been described as 'ideals', 'types' and individuals. How does Chaucer present his portraits in different ways? Make detailed reference to at least three portraits.

6 Discuss the various descriptive techniques that Chaucer uses to present the pilgrims.

7 How is vanity presented as a theme?

8 Show how greed and avarice are established as strong themes in the poem.

9 Do you agree that there is sometimes a difference between the images that the pilgrims hold of themselves, and the truth revealed of their characters in the *General Prologue*? Discuss at least three examples.

10 Which portrait appeals to you most? Explain the features that make it memorable.

11 Do you admire the vitality of the characters? To what extent is vitality established in the presentation of the characters, and is it to be admired even when put to ill use?

12 How effectively is humour established in the poem?

13 Discuss the relationship between the opening, the ending and the portraits in the poem.

14 'The good characters are unrealistically good.' How far do you agree with this statement?

15 'A duality of sacred and secular impulse.' Is this a fair description of the Prioress?

Chronology

1372–3	Chaucer on King's business in Italy
1374	Moved to Aldgate in London; appointed Customs Controller (to control taxes on wool, sheepskins and leather)
1376–7	Further travelling in Flanders and France on King's secret business. 1376 'Good Parliament' meets; death of Edward, the Black Prince. 1377 Death of Edward III; accession of Richard II
1378	Travelled again to Italy – renewed acquaintance with works of Italian writers
1378–80	*The House of Fame* written; 1379 Richard II introduces Poll Tax
1380–2	*The Parliament of Fowls*; 1381 Peasants' Revolt
1380s	Moved to Kent (precise date unknown)
1382–6	*Troilus and Criseyde* and *The Legend of Good Women* written. 1385 gave up post at Custom House; became Justice of the Peace
1386	Gave up house at Aldgate; election to Parliament
1387	Phillipa presumed to have died
1388–92	The *General Prologue* and earlier *Canterbury Tales* written; 1389–91 appointed to be Clerk of the King's works. 1391–2 *A Treatise on the Astrolabe* written
1392–5	Most of *The Canterbury Tales* completed
1396–1400	Later *Canterbury Tales* written; 1396 Anglo-French Treaty. 1397–9 Richard II's reign of 'tyranny'
1399	Returned to London, in a house near the Lady Chapel of Westminster Abbey; deposition of Richard II; accession of Henry IV
1400	Chaucer died (date on tomb in Westminster Abbey given as 25 October)

Further Reading

Editions

You may find that the following editions have useful notes:

L.D. Benson (ed.), *The Riverside Chaucer* (Oxford University Press, 1988)

F.N. Robinson (ed.), *The Works of Geoffrey Chaucer* (2nd ed.) (Oxford University Press, 1957)

Walter Skeat, *The Prologue to The Canterbury Tales* (Oxford University Press, 1890)

James Winny, *The General Prologue to The Canterbury Tales* (Cambridge University Press, 1965)

Biography

D.R. Howard, *Chaucer, His Life, His Works, His World* (Dutton, 1987)

G. Kane, *Chaucer* (Past Masters Series) (Oxford University Press, 1984)

Criticism

Michael Alexander, *Prologue to The Canterbury Tales* (Longman, 1980)

Muriel Bowden, *A Commentary on the General Prologue to The Canterbury Tales* (Macmillan, 1973)

This book in the series Oxford Guides to Chaucer provides a succinct and reliable account of recent scholarship:

Helen Cooper, *The Canterbury Tales* (Oxford University Press, 1989)

This book is still valuable on particular issues, though some of
its conclusions have been contested:
W.C. Curry, *Chaucer and the Medieval Sciences* (Barnes and
Noble, 1960)

This book has a useful commentary:
E.T. Donaldson, (ed.) *Chaucer's Poetry* (California Press, New
York, 1975)

D.R. Howard, *The Idea of The Canterbury Tales* (California Press,
London, 1985)

The controversy around the Knight may be followed up in these
two publications:
Terry Jones, *Chaucer's Knight* (Routledge, 1980)
Maurice Keen, 'Chaucer's Knight, the English Aristocracy and
the Crusade' in V.J. Scattergood and J.W. Sherborne (eds.)
English Court Culture in the Later Middle Ages (Duckworth,
1983)

This critical work revolutionized the study of the *General
Prologue*:
Jill Mann, *Chaucer and Medieval Estates Satire* (Cambridge
University Press, 1973)

Other useful books

J.D. North, *Chaucer's Universe* (Oxford University Press, 1988)
Clair C. Olson, 'Chaucer and Fourteenth-Century Society' in
Beryl Rowland (ed.) *Companion to Chaucer Studies* (Oxford
University Press, Toronto, 1968)
Derek Pearsall, *The Canterbury Tales* (Unwin, 1985)
Eileen Power, *Medieval People* (Penguin, 1924)
Paul Strohm, *Social Chaucer* (Harvard University Press, 1989)

Historical background

L.C. Lambdin and R.T. Lambdin (eds.), *Chaucer's Pilgrims: An Historical Guide* (Greenwood Press, 1996)

This book is very good on social background:
Maurice Keen, *English Society in the Later Middle Ages* (Penguin, 1990)

This book provides a very lively account of the period:
B. Tuchman, *A Distant Mirror: The Calamitous 14th Century* (Penguin, 1990)

The important topic of clothes is discussed exhaustively in:
Laura Hodges, *Chaucer and Costume: The Secular Pilgrims in the General Prologue* (D.S. Brewer, 2000)
Laura Hodges, *Chaucer and Clothing: Clerical and Academic Costume in the General Prologue* (D.S. Brewer, 2005)

This article argues that Chaucer's *General Prologue* shows a clear commitment to an aristocratic ideology in response to the Peasants' Revolt of 1381:
Alcuin Blamires, 'Chaucer the Reactionary: Ideology and the General Prologue to the Canterbury Tales', *Review of English Studies*, 51 (2000), pp. 523–39

This chapter provides texts and translations of writings Chaucer drew on in composing the *General Prologue*:
Robert R. Raymo, 'The General Prologue' in R. Correale and M. Hamel (eds.) *Sources and Analogues of the Canterbury Tales*, Volume II (D.S. Brewer, 2005), pp. 1–85

Language

D. Burnley, *A Guide to Chaucer's Language* (Macmillan, 1983)
N. Davis (ed.), *A Chaucer Glossary* (Oxford University Press, 1968)

Websites

This site gives access to a range of excellent scholarly and teaching materials on Chaucer:
www.courses.fas.harvard.edu/~chaucer/

This page of the Luminarium website gives access to a range of materials on Chaucer and a few essays on the *General Prologue*:
www.luminarium.org/medlit/chaucessays.htm

Glossary

This glossary is not absolutely comprehensive. It does not record all inflected forms (see A Note on Chaucer's English, page 149) nor all variant spellings. If you do not find a word here, try sounding it out, or try minor modifications of spelling (such as 'i' for 'y', 'a' for 'o', 'ea' for 'ee', and vice versa). A few of the glosses in the commentary are not repeated in the glossary. Generally the main meaning *in this text* comes first, while more specialized meanings are given line references. Proper names which are explained in the notes do not appear in the glossary. In compiling this glossary I have relied on L.D. Benson (ed.), *The Riverside Chaucer* and on N. Davis (ed.), *A Chaucer Glossary*, which offer fuller explanations than I can here. I have also consulted the *Oxford English Dictionary* and *The Middle English Dictionary*.

aboute around
absolucioun absolution, forgiveness of sins
accorde agreement, decision
achaat buying
achatours buyers
acord agree
acordaunt agreeing
adrad afraid
aferd afraid
affile smooth
after according to (125), towards (136)
agayn against
al although
al all, entirely
alderbest best of all
ale-stake pub-sign
algate always
als as

alwey always, continually
alyght dismounted, arrived
amblere ambling horse
amorwe in the morning
anlaas dagger
anon immediately
apes fools, dupes
apiked trimmed
apothecaries pharmacists
areste stop
arette attribute to, impute
aright certainly, exactly
array clothing, dress
arrerage arrears
arwe arrow
ascendent planet coming over the horizon
asonder apart
assoillyng absolution
astored provided

atones at one time
atte at
aught all
avaunce profit
avaunt assertion, boast
aventure chance
avys consideration
awe reverence, fear
ay always, continually

baar, bar carried, wore
bacheler apprentice knight (80)
bad asked, told
baillif farm manager
bargaynes deals (sales and
    purchases)
barge ship, sea-going merchant
    vessel
barres stripes
bataille battle
bawdryk baldric, shoulder-
    strap
bedes beads
beggestere beggar-woman
ben are
benefice church job
benygne kind, considerate
berd beard
bet better
bifalle happen (*bifil* 19)
biforn before, in front of, ahead
    (572)
bigonne began, sat at the head
    of (52)
bisette used
bisides near, in addition
bisily earnestly
bismotered bespattered
bit bids, commands
bitwixe between

blake black
blankmanger mousse (see
    Notes p. 64, line 387)
blisful happy, blessed (17)
blithe happy, pleased
bokeler small shield
boote remedy
boras borax
bord table
born hym conducted himself
bracer arm guard
brawn muscle
breem freshwater bream
breeth breath
bretful brimful
bretherhed guild, confraternity
brode plainly
brood broad, wide
broun brown, dark
brustles bristles
brymstoon sulphur
burdoun bass accompaniment
burgeys burgess, member of
    the city council
but only, except
but if unless
bynne grain bin
byte burn, scour
byynge buying

caas cases, eventuality, chance
carf carved
carl rogue
carpe talk
catel property
ceint belt
celle subordinate house
ceruce white lead
chambre bedroom
chaped mounted

chapeleyne secretary
chapman merchant
charge burden, responsibility
charitee Christian love, goodwill
chaunce event, fortune
chaunterie chantry, job singing
  masses
cheere manners, behaviour,
  expression
cherubynnes cherub's
chevyssaunce financial
  arrangements, borrowings
chiere welcome, greeting
chyvachie cavalry expedition
clad covered, clothed, bound
  (294)
cleere clearly
clene cleanly, brightly (367)
clennesse purity
clepe call, name, say (643)
clerk educated person, scholar
cloysterer monk
cloystre cloister
cofre coffer, money-chest
colerik choleric (see Notes p.
  60, line 333)
colpons strands
compeer companion
complexioun temperament (see
  Notes p. 60, line 333)
composicioun agreement
condicioun state, circumstances
conseil secrets, decision (784)
contour auditor
contree district
cop tip
cope long cloak, cape
coppe cup
corage courage, heart, spirit,
  inclination

cordial medicine for the heart
cosyn closely related
cote tunic, coat
countrefete imitate
cours course
courtepy jacket
covenaunt agreement, contract
coverchiefs headcoverings
covyne deceit
coy quiet
craft skill, profession
cristen Christian
cristendom Christendom,
  Christian countries
croppes shoots (of plants)
croys cross
crulle curled
cryke creek, inlet
curat parish priest
cure care
curious skilful, skilfully made
curteis courteous
curteisie courtesy, good
  manners
cut lot

daliaunce sociable talk, flirting
daunce dance
daunger control (663)
daungerous haughty, aloof
dayerye dairy cattle
decree decretal, law of the
  church
deed dead
degree rank, social class
delit delight, pleasure
delve dig
delyvere agile
desdeyn indignation
despitous scornful

desport amusement
dettelees without debts
devout pious
devys scheme, wishes
devyse tell
deyntee fine, superior
deyntees delicacies
deys dais
digne worthy, haughty (517)
dischevelee with hair unbound
discreet judicious
disport entertainment
dokked cut short
dong dung
doomes judgements
dormant permanently in place
dorste dared
double worstede thick, expensive cloth
draughte draught, the quantity of liquid taken at one swallow
dresse arrange, care for, prepare
drogges drugs
droghte drought
drouped fell short
dyke make ditches
dyvyne divine, holy

ecclesiaste churchman
ech each
eek also
embrouded embroidered
encombred stuck
endite write poetry (95), draft documents (325)
engendred produced
enoynt anointed, rubbed with oil
ensample example
entuned intoned

envyned stocked with wine
er before
ercedekenes archdeacon's
erly early
erst first
erys ears
eschaunge exchange, market
ese comfort, pleasure
estaat condition, position in society
estatly, estatlich dignified
esy lenient
esy of dispence moderate in spending
evene moderate
everichon everyone, all
everemoore always
everydeel every part, altogether
excellence exceptional talent

facultee professional dignity
faire well, beautifully, handsomely, neatly
faldyng coarse woollen cloth
famulier familiar
farsed stuffed
fayn gladly
fee symple absolute possession
felawe companion
felaweshipe fellowship
felicitee happiness
fer far, at a distance
ferme fee, rent
ferne distant
ferre farther
ferther further
ferthyng farthing (quarter-penny), drop (134)
festne fasten
fetisly elegantly

feyne invent
fille fell
fithele fiddle
Flaundres Flanders
flessh meat
flex flax
flour flower
flour-de-lys lily
floytynge playing the flute
foo foe, enemy, opponent
foot-mantel overskirt
forneys furnace, oven, fire (202)
forpyned tormented
forster forester
fortunen calculate
forward agreement
fother cartload
foweles birds
frankeleyn free man,
　landowner
fraternitee confraternity, guild
fredom generosity, nobleness
fressh new, young, blooming,
　vigorous
fro from
ful very
fustian coarse cloth

galyngale a root used in
　flavouring
game sport
gat-tothed with teeth set wide
　apart
gauded with large beads
gay finely dressed, splendid,
　bright
geere equipment, cutlery (352)
gentil noble
gerland garland
gerner granary

gesse suppose, perceive
gipser purse
girdle belt
girt encircled
gise manner
glarynge staring
gobet piece
goliardeys buffoon, joker
good wealth, property (611)
goon go
goost spirit
governaunce behaviour, rule,
　control
graunt agree
graunt grant, privilege
grece grease
gretter larger
grope test, question
ground texture
grounded instructed
grys squirrel-fur
gyde guide
gynglen jingle
gypon tunic

haberdasshere haberdasher,
　seller of clothing accessories
habergeon coat of mail
halwe saint, shrine (14)
hardily certainly
hardy brave, tough
harlot rascal
harlotries indecency
harm misfortune, pain, pity
　(385)
harneised mounted,
　ornamented
harre hinge
haunt practice, skill (447), usual
　place (252b)

havenes harbours (407)
heed head
heede notice (303)
heeld held, considered, followed (176)
heep lot, crowd
heeth heath, open land
hem them
hente obtain
herberwe shelter, lodging, harbour (403), inn (765)
herkneth listen
hertely cordially
herys hairs
hethenesse heathen countries
hewe colour
hierde herdsman
highte called
hir their
hir, hire her
hire money, payment
holden considered
holp help
holt wood
holwe hollow, emaciated
hond hand, wrist
honest honourable, respectable
hoole whole
hoomly simply
hoote hotly, passionately
hosen stockings
hostelrye inn
hostiler innkeeper
humour type of bodily fluid
hy serious
hyndreste last
hyne servant

ilke same
infect invalidated

inspire breathe life into (6)
iren iron

janglere chatterer, teller of tales
japes tricks
jet fashion
jolitee ease
juste joust
justice judge

kan knows
keep, kep notice (in the phrase 'take keep')
kepe take care of, preserve, ensure (130), protect (276)
kepere supervisor
knarre rugged fellow
knyght of the shire member of parliament representing the county
knobbes lumps
koude knew (how to)
kouthe could
kowthe known

laas cord
large freely (734)
lat let
latoun latten, brass
lazar leper
leed cauldron
leet allowed, let
lene lean
lengthe height (83)
lest desire, pleasure
letuaries electuaries, medicines
levere rather
lewed ignorant
licenciat licensed

licour liquid
lipsed lisped
liste wanted, preferred (often used impersonally)
lite little, small
lodemenage pilotage
lond land
loore teaching
lordynges sirs, gentlemen
love-dayes days on which disputes were resolved
lowely humble, modest
luce pike
lust pleasure, delight
lusty lively
lymytour limiter (see Notes p. 52, line 209)
lystes lists, venue for tournaments
lytarge lead monoxide
lyveree uniform (of the guild 363)

maistrie mastery, control
maladye illness
male bag
maner sort
manhod manliness
mantel cloak
marchal master of ceremonies
martir martyr
marybones marrow bones
maunciple business agent
medlee parti-coloured
meede meadow
meeke meek, humble
mercenarie hireling
mere mare
meschief trouble
mesurable moderate

mete food, mealtime
mo more
mormal ulcer, running sore
mortreux thick soup or stew
morwe morning
mottelee cloth of mixed colour
moyste supple
muchel much
murierly more pleasantly
murye merry, pleasing
muwe pen for birds
myght power
myre mire, bog
myrthe mirth, amusement, happiness
myscarie come to grief
myster trade

namoore no more
narwe narrow
nas was not
nat not
nathelees nevertheless
ne not, and... not, nor
neet cattle
noght not, not at all, nothing
nones occasion
noot do not know
norissyng nourishment
nosethirles nostrils
not heed close-cropped head
note voice
nowthe now
ny near, close
nyce scrupulous
nyghtertale night-time

o one
office secular job

offrynge offering, collection
  (450), priest's income from
  collection (489)
oille of tartre cream of tartar
oon one
oon, after uniformly good
ooth oath
ounces small strands
outrely absolutely
outridere outrider, monk with
  business outside the
  monastery
over al everywhere
overeste uppermost
over-lippe upper lip
overspradde covered
owher anywhere
oynement ointment

paas walking speed (825)
pace go, surpass (574)
palfrey horse
pardee by God, to be sure
parfit perfect
parisshens parishioners
partrich partridge
pass go, pass by, surpass
patente letter of appointment
peire set
penaunce penance (see Notes
  to the Pardoner, p. 80)
perced pierced
pers grey-blue
persoun parson
pestilence plague
peyned hire took pains
phisik medicine
piled hairless
pilwe-beer pillowcase
pitaunce gift, payment

pitous compassionate
plentevous abundant
pleyen to play
pleyn full, entirely
pomely dappled
poraille poor people
port manner, behaviour
post pillar
pouch purse
poudre-marchant tart a sharp-
  flavoured spice
poure pore over
povre poor
poynaunt sharp, spicy
poynt condition
praktisour practitioner
prelaat prelate, high-ranking
  churchman
presse cupboard, curler (81),
  casting mould (263)
prikasour hunter
priketh spurs, stimulates
prikyng tracking
pris, prys value, reputation,
  price (815), prize (237)
propre own
proprely appropriately,
  correctly
pryvely secretly
pulled plucked
purchace buy property
purchas income
purchasour land-buyer
purfiled lined with fur
purtreye draw, describe
pynche at find an error in
pynched pleated

quyk vivid (306)
quyk-silver mercury

rage sport, frolic
raughte reached
recchelees careless
recorde remind, recall
rede read, interpret (741)
reed red
reed advisor (665)
reeve estate manager
reherce repeat
rekene reckon, calculate
rekenynge account
remenaunt remainder
rennyng running
rente rent, income
reportour record keeper
resoun reason
reverence respect, dignity,
   ceremony (525)
reysed ridden on raids
riche richly (609)
roialliche royally, splendidly
rood rode
roost roast
roote root, cause
rote stringed instrument
rote, by by heart
rouncy horse, carthorse
route company
rudeliche crudely

sangwyn sanguine (see Notes p.
   60, line 333), red (439)
saucefleem pimpled
saugh saw
sautrie psaltery (a stringed
   instrument, like a small harp)
save apart from
scalled scabby
scarsly economically
scathe pity

science knowledge
sclendre thin
scoleye attend university
see sea
seege siege
seeke sick (18)
seigh saw
seke, seche seek
semely beautiful, comely,
   elegant(ly)
semycope short cloak
semyly properly (151)
sendal thin silk
sentence meaning, significance
servysable attentive, willing to
   serve
sessiouns law courts, court
   hearings
sethe simmer
shamefastnesse modesty
shapen yow intend
shaply suitable, fit
sheeld écu, unit of exchange
   (see Notes p. 55, line 278)
sheene bright
shire county
shirreve sheriff
shiten filthy
sho shoe
shoures showers
shyne shin
sike sick
sikerly certainly, surely
sire master
sithes times
slee kill
sleighte tricks
smerte suffer (230), painfully
   (149)
smoot beat

177

smothe smoothly
sobrely gravely, seriously
solaas delight
solempne dignified
solempnely ceremoniously,
    pompously
somdel somewhat
somtyme once
sondry various
sonne sun
soore severely, bitterly
soote sweet, fragrant
soothly truly
sop piece of bread
soper supper
sort luck
soun sound
souple supple
Southwerk Southwark
sownynge sounding, agreeing
    with (see Notes p. 55, line 275)
space time, opportunity, course
    (176)
spak spoke
spanne span, about 18–23 cm
spare refrain, hold back
sparwe sparrow
speede prosper
spiced delicate, over-particular
spores spurs
sprynge break, begin
stature height
stemed gleamed
stepe prominent, bright
stif strong
stoor livestock
stot horse
stout strong
straunge foreign
streit strict, narrow

streite tightly
strem river, current (402)
strike hank
stronde shore
studieth deliberate, brood,
    study
stuwe fishpond
stywardes stewards
substaunce wealth, pay (489)
subtilly cunningly
suffisaunce sufficiency
suffre allow
superfluitee excess
surcote outer coat
swerd sword
swetely gently, in a kindly
    manner
swich such
swyn pigs
swynk work
symple unaffected, innocent
syn since

tabard loose upper garment
Tabard the Tabard inn
taffata taffeta, a type of silk
taille, by on credit
takel equipment
talen tell stories
tappestere barmaid
tapycer weaver of tapestries
    and rugs
targe shield
taryynge delay
temple Inn of Court, lawyers'
    college
tendre tender, young
termes law reports (323),
    expressions (639)
thanne then

ther there, where
theron on it
therto to it, about it, in addition, also
thilke that same
tho those
thries three times
thriftily properly, carefully
til to
tithe tenth, proportion due to the Church
toft tuft
tollen charge, take payment
tretys well-formed
trompe trumpet
trouthe fidelity, loyalty, honour
trowe believe
trussed packed
tukked hitched up
tweye two
twynne part, go
typet point of the hood

undergrowe small, underdeveloped
undertake declare
untrewe falsely, inaccurately
usage customs

vavasour sub-vassal (sse Notes p. 61, line 360)
venerie hunting
vernycle badge from the pilgrimage to Rome
verray true
vertu power (4)
vertuous virtuous, capable
veyne vein
viage voyage, journey
vigilies, vigils services and feasts held the night before holy days
vileynye boorishness, vulgarity, rude words (70)
visage face
vitaille victuals, provisions
voirdit verdict
vouche sauf agree

wait (wayte) expect, take care (571)
walet travel bag
wantowne jolly, pleasure-loving
wantownesse affectation
war aware, prudent (309)
wastel-breed fine white bread
webbe weaver
weel well
wende go
werk do
werre war
werte wart
wex wax
weye road, journey
weyeden weighed
whan when
whelkes pimples
whelp puppy
wherwith the wherewithal, (money) with which
whilom once, formerly
wight man
wiste knew, expected
wit intelligence
withholde retained, employed
withouten not counting
wodecraft woodcraft, forestry, gamekeeping
wol will
wolde wanted, would

wonderly marvellously
wone custom
wonyng living, dwelling
wood mad
woot know
worthy deserving, respectable, distinguished
wrighte workman
wroghte made, did
wrooth angry
wyde wide, spacious (28), large (491)
wympul wimple, garment covering the whole head but leaving the face visible
wynne earn money
wynnyng earnings, profit
wys wise, prudent

yaf gave
ydrawe drawn, taken

ye eye
yeddynges ballads
yeldehalle guildhall
yeldynge yield
yemanly skilfully, in a yeomanly fashion
yerde stick
yeve give
yfalle fallen
ygo gone
yive give
ylad hauled
ymage talisman (418)
ynogh enough
yonge young
yronne run
yshadwed shaded
yteyd laced, tied
ywympled covered with a wimple
ywroght made

Appendix

History of the Destruction of Troy

Guido delle Colonne completed his Latin prose *History of the Destruction of Troy* in 1287. Chaucer certainly knew it and used some details from it in his long poem on the Troy legend, *Troilus and Criseyde* (completed about 1385). Compare this translated passage from the beginning of Guido's fourth book with the first sentence of the *General Prologue*.

> It was the time when the sun... had already begun its journey through the sign of Aries, when the spring equinox is celebrated, when the weather begins to entice eager mortals into the clear fresh air. At that time the ice has broken and the mildly blowing West wind ripples the waters, the springs begin to flow, the moisture exhaled from the earth is drawn up to treetops and the tips of branches. From these the seeds sprout, the seedlings grow, the meadows become green, adorned with the different coloured flowers. The trees all around send forth new leaves, the earth is covered in grass, the birds sing and make music in the modulation of sweet harmony. Then almost half the month of April has passed...

> (translated from Guido delle Colonne's *Historia destructionis Troiae* ed. N.E. Griffin [1936])

Roman de la Rose

The *Roman de la Rose*, an Old French poem and one of the most influential works of the later Middle Ages, sets out in allegorical form the whole art of love. The poem was begun around 1237 by the courtly poet Guillaume de Lorris. About 40 years after

Appendix

Guillaume's death the scholar Jean de Meun vastly enlarged and completed the work in a somewhat earthier style. Chaucer himself made a translation of the *Roman de la Rose* (called *The Romaunt of the Rose*) and its influence has been traced in many of his works.

The first translated extract is a description of a May morning from the beginning of the poem. Compare this with the opening sentence of the *General Prologue*.

> I realised that it was May, a good five years ago, or even more. I dreamed that we were in May, the joyful time of love, the time when everyone is happy, when every bush and hedge is covered with new leaves. The woods, which are so dry while winter lasts, recover their green. The earth itself becomes proud because of the dew which waters it, and forgets the poverty it has been in all winter. When the earth becomes so vain that it wants to have a new dress with a hundred pairs of colours in the grass, and the flowers of blue, white and other colours... The birds which were silent and cold in the bitter weather of winter are so joyful because of the fair weather of May. They feel compelled to sing in order to show how much joy they have in their hearts. The nightingales must sing loudly; the parrot and lark revive and satiate themselves in joy. The joyous beautiful weather makes young men feel themselves happy and amorous. The person who does not feel love in May, when he hears the sweet piteous songs of the birds on their branches, has a very hard heart. (45–83)

The second translated extract is from Jean de Meun's continuation. La Vieille, an older and somewhat cynical woman, is explaining the part played in the art of seduction by table manners. Compare Chaucer's description of the Prioress at table (127–136).

> Let her take care never to dip her fingers deeply (as far as the joint) into the sauce, never to cover her lips in soup, garlic or fat, never to take too large a morsel, or stuff too much in her

mouth. When she has to dip a piece of meat in the sauce, of whatever kind, she should hold it with her fingertips and carry it carefully to her mouth, so that no drop of soup, sauce or pepper falls on her breast. Let her drink so carefully that she spills nothing on herself. Anyone seeing her spill her drink might think her ill-educated or greedy. She must not touch her glass while she has food in her mouth. She should wipe her lips clean, especially the upper lip, because if any grease remains there, drops of it will appear in her wine, which is ugly and dirty. (13408–32)

(translated from Guillaume de Lorris and Jean de Meun's *Le Roman de la Rose* ed. D. Poirion [Paris, 1974])

Piers Plowman

Piers Plowman is a Middle English allegorical poem composed in four versions (known as Z, A, B and C) by William Langland between about 1362 and 1390. The prologue to *Piers Plowman* contains a description of fourteenth-century English society which may be placed beside Chaucer's *General Prologue*. The continuous extract from Walter Skeat's edition of the B text, printed below, includes Langland's discussions of the friars, a pardoner and corrupt parish priests. Similar material appears in Chaucer's accounts, and it is possible that an early version of *Piers Plowman* was among Chaucer's sources. Compare the attitude of the observer in *Piers Plowman* to that of the pilgrim Chaucer (208–69, 496–514, 669–714). In what way are Langland's criticisms of parish priests reflected in Chaucer's praise of his Parson?

> I fonde there freris alle the foure ordres,
> Preched the peple for profit of hem-selven,
> 60 Glosed the gospel as hem good lyked,
> For coveitise of copis construed it as thei wolde.
> Many of this maistres freris mowe clothen hem at lykyng,
> For here money and marchandise marchen togideres.

> For sith charite hath be chapman and chief to shryve
> lordes,
> 65 Many ferlis han fallen in a fewe yeris.
> Bot holychirche and hii holde better togideres,
> The moste myschief on molde is mountyng wel faste.

60 **Glosed** commented on, explained 63 **marchandise** business
64 **chapman** businessman **shryve** give confession to 65 **ferlis**
wonders 67 **myschief** harm **molde** earth

> There preched a pardonere as he a prest were,
> Broughte forth a bulle with bishopes seles,
> 70 And seide that hym-self myghte assoilen hem alle
> Of falshed of fastyng of vowes ybroken.
> Lewed men leved hym wel and lyked his wordes,
> Comen up knelyng to kissen his bulles;
> He bonched hem with his brevet and blered here eyes,
> 75 And raughte with his ragman rynges and broches.
> Thus they geven here golde glotones to kepe,
> And leveth such loseles that lecherye haunten.
> Were the bischop yblissed and worth bothe his eres,
> His seel shulde nought be sent to deceyve the peple.
> 80 Ac it is naught by the bischop that the boy precheth,
> For the parisch prest and the pardonere parten the silver,
> That the poraille of the parisch sholde have if thei nere.

69 **bulle** document 70 **assoilen** absolve 72 **Lewed** ignorant
leved believed 74 **bonched** struck **brevet** letter of indulgence
blered dimmed 75 **raughte** obtained **ragman** document 77
loseles rascals **haunten** indulge in 80 **boy** rogue

> Persones and parisch prestes pleyned hem to the bischop,
> That here parisshes were pore sith the pestilence tyme,
> 85 To have a lycence and a leve at London to dwelle,
> And syngen there for symonye for silver is swete.
> Bischopes and bachelers bothe maistres and doctours,
> That han cure under Criste and crounyng in tokne
> And signe that thei sholden shryven here paroschienes,
> 90 Prechen and prey for hem and the pore fede,